THE EXISTENTIALIST CRAVES NONBEING

Apathy, Dread, Self-hatred, and Philosophical Pessimism

J. GUZMÁN

D1452811

Loner Girl Press

For permissions and collaborations contact j@jguzman.space

You can connect with the author on Instagram @jguzmanwriter. Visit her website at jguzman.space and join her mailing list under the Contact tab.

to the Master of my nativity

I admit I am powerless to you.
How can I appease you, my Lord?

for astrological purposes

𝄞

Ana Ebtz
14 January 1991
8:42 a.m.
Lewiston, ID, USA

𝄞

The Existentialist Craves Nonbeing
(eBook version)
28 August 2020
8:02 a.m.
Meridian, ID, USA

𝄞

THE EXISTENTIALIST CRAVES
NONBEING

02 September 2010

I went to the Seattle Art Museum today with Mila and Eugenia. I got to see Kurt Cobain one last time because the exhibit is still up. I thought the last time would be before summer, but I was wrong. Delighted!

I can't believe I'm here. I never want to go back to Boise, I can't do it. I need to live here somehow. I will if it's the last thing I do.

I want to know where Kurt and Courtney met, and I want to go to all the places that all the interesting people go to. I feel like there's some secret place where everything happens, and I don't know about it. Like everyone's part of some exclusive and exciting club and I'm left out.

Being in Seattle helps a lot, but I still get this strange feeling that I'm missing something crucial, and I'm always going to search for it. I hate it and I love it and it's everything I am.

03 September 2010

Listening to the new Arcade Fire album, *The Suburbs*. I like "Modern Man." Drinking coffee. Going to Hawaii tomorrow for soccer!

05 September 2010

We flew to Hawaii yesterday. I sat between my parents on the plane. They are coming to watch us play and also to have a mini vacation.

I finished reading *1984* and started *The Tao of Pooh*. I'm trying to really feel each moment that I'm in. It's hard.

We swam in the ocean yesterday. It's within walking distance of our hotel. We also went to the market and I bought bracelets to give to my friends. Today we had practice and went to the beach. It's real hot. I'm icing my ankle right now on our balcony. Breezy.

There was this sexy guy at the beach with long hair and my teammates started talking to him about me so I ran away. Swam away, actually. So touristy here, kinda annoying. We are going to dinner soon.

There are so many things in the world, so many tiny things I'll never see. Like cigarette butts in dark alleys and the bottom of the ocean. It's hard to concentrate on writing when I should be looking at everything. It's amazing how magical our natural world is, but we're so trapped by concrete to notice its intense beauty. There are heavy clouds resting on the mountaintops to the left of our balcony. Light gray darkens into deep blue. Mysterious.

I imagine I'm sitting in the shrouded wetness, an explorer, a sojourner of secrets. The whole relationship between the night, the clouds, and the mountains is so sublime. I can't express how I feel and I have this urge to scream and cry because of my inadequate vocabulary. My incompetence astounds me. You have six different ways you can experience this profound experiment. Take advantage of it. Be your senses.

06 September 2010

We won today, I did not have fun. I felt like the entire time I was following one girl around trying to defend her and never getting the ball or doing anything. It sucks. But that's what Chadwick wants me to do in the midfield: focus on someone else instead of trying to be a playmaker and actually helping my teammates. I also had a breakaway and kicked it right at the keeper.

Cameron played so fucking well. I'm eternally jealous of her. She is seriously the most perfect person ever; she is good at everything. I wish I were her. And since I can't be her I'll just be in love with her. And watch how she does things and secretly copy her. And stare at her with a straight face, trying to look serious and not smile because that may give away how much I idolize her.

She'll never know how I honestly think she is the coolest person ever. I don't just say that because it's true in a certain moment. I say it because it's always real and it's how I feel when I'm serious. Maybe I'm glad she doesn't know for sure because I can pretend we're good friends and we know things about each other even when we don't. I can act like she thinks I'm interesting and we've had deep conversations about life and she values me as a person even if I'm useless.

I'm drinking coffee in our room. It's around 10:15 p.m.

Mila and I walked to the beach today and read and talked and sat in the sun. It was nice. How quickly Hawaii will be in the past, lost in memories insignificant but for those moments where I long for things that will never be mine, and loathe the futility of disliking myself in the present.

We are always existing, we are never *not*, so it gets old and we forget how insane it all is. We forget how intensely gorgeous every action, thought, feeling, moment is. Even me lying here writing this wispy mind-trail down in black ink is more complicated than I can be aware of. Ever. It's important and private and genuine and dumb.

I hate when people make statements about other people in the form of factual expressions. Because who are you to say how another person is? You don't know the inside of her mind, how she operates, her rationality. You cannot say how a person is because no one is constant. We are in flux, morphing relevant ideas into blasphemous heresies from one day to the next. Nothing, nobody, is something. We are all everything, yet nothing.

Now I'm talking in vague generalities. Do you think this is worthy of publication? I don't.

I hate when people have expectations of me and I end up disappointing them. It's the worst and it happens all the time.

If I'm not beautiful how can anyone love me?

10 September 2010

The day before yesterday I only played for ten minutes in the first half of our game. I played better than the first game, though. I hate Chadwick. He doesn't say what he is thinking, he just takes me out of the game and looks at me condescendingly with those stupid thinly pursed lips, like I made some huge mistake out of something so simple, and yet says nothing. I hate him so much. It's a secret I like but don't keep very well.

Yesterday I went snorkeling with my parents at Hanauma Bay. It was so cool! I saw huge fish and scraped myself on the coral. I bought two postcards and some fake tats at the gift shop via Mom's debit card. We went to another beach, too, with turquoise water and sand so fine it was like liquid. Not too many people either. So much better than Waikiki. We went out to lunch and to various lookouts. I took a bunch of pictures.

Our team went to a Luau last night: food and dancing, hilarious. We made our assistant coach go up and dance, he wore a coconut bra and no shirt. Funniest thing ever! I bought our team pic for ten dollars. Practice today was short but I did awful. Felt sluggish and bloated.

I wonder if I will keep thinking of a million more things to say in my life. I wonder if I'll wonder about anything new, sense a different mysterious than the usual pondering. I think that's kind of interesting. I want to grow my hair out. I am, it's getting longer. When it's long I'll be the same person. Will I be happier? Will I change? It might as well be long right now because I'll probably have the same mindset as I do now.

13 September 2010

I am so satisfied right now. BEST FEELING EVER. Everything is perfect. The atmosphere I occupy consists of: an unpacked and organized dorm room, alone, warm, dim lights, tea, iPod on shuffle, freshly showered body, everything in the right place, excitement! I think this year is going to be fucking great. My room is really spacious compared to last year. I love how much space I have. Comfort. I can't wait for Zara to get here so our room can be complete. It's bare on her side.

I packed all my shit into Claire's car and she helped me move into my dorm. It didn't take long at all. Painless, unlike the confused awkwardness of last year. Since we live on the top floor we parked behind the building because there is a parking lot at the top, so no elevator or stairs with all my crap.

I also talked to my PA, the girl that kind of manages and looks out for everyone on our floor. It was totally fine, she's real nice. She is black and has short pixie hair and is pretty.

We won our last game in Hawaii at the end of double over-time. I assisted Bridgette and she scored but they said it was offside, and a little later Sierra scored and we won.

15 September 2010

Downtown. Went to the public library with 40 minutes till closing. Worst decision ever. What a waste of bus fare.

How do I know which people are real? How do I know which people are creepy and scary? Because there are creepy and scary looking people that are actually real and brilliant. How do I sort those from the shitty ones?

I'm sitting on the ground at the bus stop. I've never sat on the ground downtown anywhere, it's what the homeless do. I want to do it more often.

I went to Fremont today and bought *The Fountainhead* for $3.83. One of the freshmen named Kate bought me a Kurt Cobain poster at Pike's; she gave it to me at dinner. Sex. Kate is so nice, she is short and blonde and plays defense, and likes good music and is really quiet. I like her.

I might be the coolest person I know. (What a fucking stupid thing to write.) It's 11:04 p.m. I'm drinking tea in a red teacup. It's raining outside. I want to work at a bookstore. I'm tired. Tomorrow we have a game.

I'm wondering if Seattle's right. If anywhere is right. How can I know if it's right if I haven't seen everything else? It rained today and I liked it. I felt sad a little, like something's missing, but I liked it. I wonder if I enjoy feeling this way for some reason. I wonder if something will always be missing. My feelings are so obscure. I can never figure myself out.

I need to do things I've never done, occupy spaces in strange positions, say things that can be interpreted in various ways. I always want to have an adventure, but when I actually think about it, I wonder if it would just make me super anxious and afraid of the people that want me to come.

17 September 2010

I played really well in our game yesterday. It was like the old me finally returned! Fuckin' insane. Best I've ever played here. I'm scared because Cameron and another midfielder aren't playing tomorrow so I'm starting at center mid and I'm afraid I'll fuck it up. Oh well. I'm just going to play and not think. And hope it works out.

19 September 2010

Yesterday the game was okay. I was hella tired but it was okay. I didn't majorly fuck anything up so that was good, and we won 2-0. I got to go home since our game was in Boise. I

7

showered and iced my injuries and ate healthy. I'm glad I got to visit with my parents, too. I'm already back in Seattle. Zara got here yesterday but didn't move all her stuff in till today.

I went to the Sunday market in Fremont with a hilarious freshman named Kendra and a few of the junior girls. Kendra plays forward and is super fast. We went to the junior girls' new house, which they call The Brick because it's made of brick, and then we visited the junior guys' house, which is behind my dorm and up the hill a bit, really close. I'm totes going to go over there all the time!

20 September 2010

1:08 a.m. School starts next Monday.

I looked in the mirror and became very depressed. Reading poetry by Charles Bukowski is like seeing my soul etched in blackness on smooth paper. It's good, it makes me want to write in these short, choppy sentences, even when I'm tired and don't want to think.

Don't want there to be a tomorrow or practice or bloatedness or anything. I wanna be a fuck-up. I've been obeying these stupid fucking rules. I'm going to be sick and vulgar and truthful and instinctual, and I'm gonna do it wrong because there is no wrong and that's how it goes.

These are the things I don't tell people: I want Cameron. I want to see something die. I am scared of insanity taking over and I want it to because I've been trying so hard to fend it off for so long. I just want to give up, all the time. I'm a liar and I always tell the truth. I want to do drugs and starve on the streets because there's nothing better. I don't want to be afraid of things that aren't clean or aligned correctly.

I need someone and I pretend that I don't. I hate myself. I laugh a lot because I'm happy. I don't like being portrayed as a happy person, it annoys the fuck out of me. I feel things and other people don't get it. I'm self-absorbed. I'm awkward and jealous and I hate it, but I love it because I imagine someone loving me because of those qualities, the way I have loved others in secret because they have those characteristics as well.

24 September 2010

Laying on the hotel room floor. We had an away game yesterday and won 3-1. I played a lot, I played all right.

I've discovered I'm in love with the band White Lies. I already knew this, but on the bus the other day to our game I was listening to them, and I felt this deep security for a moment in my heart. Where you expect love to be when it's real and you know it's real, and you're safe from all the shit and everything's right. And you can finally just rest and be in the moment you're in and be content with the situation you're in.

I felt all this for, like, a second, and it was the guy's voice that sparked the feeling. It was so strange.

27 September 2010

Lots to say. Today was the first day of school. I felt hot and sweaty all day.

Soccer was stupid. I HATE Chadwick. We had weight room workout right after class. Chadwick thought I was going to hurt myself because I wasn't wearing our team's designated running shoes. Instead I was wearing other closed-toe shoes

9

that are totally fine to wear while doing the weight room. They are like slip-on tennis shoes, very comfortable, normal, close-toed. Nothing crazy. They aren't, like, ballet flats, so I don't know what the problem was.

He was asking me a million questions while I was trying to focus on doing the exercises, and he tried to make me stop doing the exercises while I was in the middle of doing them. I just wanted to scream STOP TALKING TO ME!! I can do the exercises without hurting myself! It would actually be really hard to hurt yourself doing the exercises, like, I could do them without shoes on, so fuck *off*. He is the biggest fucking asshole and he won't ever leave me alone. I loathe him. I feel like I'm always in trouble for the tiniest details that are completely insignificant and have no effect on anything.

I had a hat trick in our game on the 25th. So many people congratulated me, I felt like I didn't deserve it. I feel like I was just in the right place at the right time. We went to a party that night. It was lame because I couldn't drink or smoke. Dry season.

Today I was always rushing, it sucked. I didn't know what to do with myself either.

28 September 2010

I just want to avoid everyone and I keep seeing people I know and it's so irritating.

I AM A CHAPTER IN TIME'S BIOGRAPHY.

01 October 2010

I'm in my parent's hotel room. My hair is pink, orange, blue, and purple. Kendra helped me dye it. I swear she is the funniest person I know.

We lost our game last night and Sierra disappeared. Apparently she's taking a break, no one knows what's happening. Chadwick was being a huge asshole to her during our game and was interrogating her about why she wasn't playing as well as she can, and she had a panic attack, I think. Or just broke down. I dunno, in one moment she was just gone. He was really aggressive about it, tilting his stupid bird-head, knitting his eyebrows, frowning as if trying to solve some difficult puzzle. Fuck him. If only he knew how fake he looked, trying to feign genuine concern.

Today's Friday. School all week, it wasn't bad. My classes start at 10 and 11:30 a.m. so I can stay up late and sleep in. It feels like summer or real life. I've been worrying about the future, about getting a job, about living in Seattle. It's stupid because it's irrelevant right now.

Today we had a huge talk in the locker room about giving everything we have, and…and I just don't know. Because in the games I try. I do okay, but I just don't really care. Like, I fucking hate practice. I hate the pointless drills we do and I hate Chadwick's ignorant ideas about defending and I hate when I mess up. I'm sick of caring about it because I've tried so hard for so long and it has never worked out for me. So now I play and when I don't feel like working hard I do the least I can to get by.

I guess I feel like a fake. Because I'm there, a part of the team, but on the inside I don't give a shit about winning and losing and playing a full 90 minutes or starting the game, or anything. I just don't want to be alienated and harassed by Chadwick for not doing things his way. All I want is to be a real person and have enough money to get by and maybe be involved with a guy on occasion. And have my own place, my own thing.

I don't think I'll ever be able to believe in anything, or love anybody, for more than an hour. I swear to god. For some reason I keep thinking about honor, values, a moral code, and making the world a better place. I feel so guilty sometimes because I feel like I should have these things, do these things, but I just don't care enough. The world's going to shit and I'm just sitting here drenched in apathy.*

[*Ana: The world was always shit, you're just starting to see it for what it really is. And by "world" I think what we both mean is society and its man-made structures, not the natural world of life force energy. –J.]

03 October 2010

We tied our game yesterday, I played okay. Before our game I walked around downtown with my parents and people looked at me and commented on my hair and it was cool. Mom bought me a book called *Zen Mind, Beginner's Mind* by Shunryu Suzuki. I've been wanting to read it and am very excited!

04 October 2010

I am in the worst mood ever. I don't want to go to this school anymore. I hate Chadwick more than anything interacting with my existence, ever. He is the worst coach in the entire world; he emotionally mindfucks us. He is so manipulative and insidious and subtly aggressive.

I can't go back to Idaho because I feel trapped there, but I don't want to go here again, and I can't afford UW because

I'm not a resident of Washington. I am so depressed. There is no point to life when I'm not enjoying it. I'm not enjoying it! IF I DON'T LIKE DOING SOMETHING, I SHOULDN'T DO IT. I shouldn't push through it to prove a point, to prove that I'm strong or that I can deal with it. Lose the fucking pride. Don't do what you don't want to do. Find your niche! Find your place. Don't endure it if it isn't fun and makes you miserable.

I was thinking about why I don't like some people even if they are nice and like cool things and good music. I think it's strange how that works. I think a lot of the time people I would think are cool I don't like because *they* think they are super cool. I think I'm attracted to people that are humble and honest and genuine, and sometimes self-deprecating. I don't like people that appear too confident or that brag or act like they know everything. I don't know why.

Maybe it's because they make me feel bad about myself because I have low self-esteem, or make me feel like I'm not as good at life as they are. I am wondering if I just don't see myself in people like that so I automatically close up when I'm around them and don't trust them. I can't figure out if there is ever a legitimate reason to not like someone. Because we're all equal and important and human beings.

Is it just when your personalities don't match up? Is that a justifiable reason? Or if someone is bitchy? But is it his fault if he is? Or is it chemicals in the brain or a combo of other factors he can't control, like the way his parents treated him as a child? It's our humanity that we are, and we are all everyone else so we should love each other. Maybe we can dislike qualities in another person but not the actual person? Why am I even thinking about this right now?*

[*Ana: You're thinking about this right now so that I can tell you from the future that astrology can help you answer these kinds of questions. It's all energy exchanges between archetypal mythical figures, duality, mirroring. –J.]

06 October 2010

I've been realizing more and more that I don't want to go here next year, and that maybe I should start being a real person and doing something with my life instead of being scared to make changes. I decided I want to transfer to a university in Idaho and do a study abroad thing in, like, England, or something. I just don't like the people at this university. There aren't very many of them, first of all, and second, they're all squares. Christian squares. There's no worse combination!

I think this whole time I've just been trying to push through it and enjoy soccer when I really don't and trying to get along with boring Jesus-ness. I never really realized that I am a real fucking person! I can do whatever I want to do! I don't have to please everyone. I can make my own decisions and go wherever I want. It's amazing how I've never felt this before. Truly. Like, really, it's fucking ridiculous. Am I a complete idiot?

I was always thinking I can start doing my own thing, having my own life, when soccer is over and I'm out of college. But then I realized that college is where you make connections, meet people, do whatever you want, when you want. And I can't do this when no one is interested in the same things as me and when I am always on a strict schedule that determines what I eat and how much alcohol I'm allowed to drink. It just sucks.

It would be okay if I actually liked soccer, you know? But I don't. I think I've just hated it this whole time, and it's awful. I want it to change. I cannot see myself going through this shit for two more years after this. That would be horrible. I think I'll feel so free after I do this, and I think it'll be really weird. Also, I feel bad for leaving my teammates. I think they are the only reason I want to stay because I feel like I'm disappointing them or not caring enough to help them out. But, it's not about them, it's about me. It's my life.

I think the main thing that I don't want to leave is the city. My beloved. My dirty, loyal, cold-hearted lover. Safe and terrifying in the same moment. I'll miss her so fucking badly. They'll have to tear me away, and it will be painful. Unbearable. I'm not sure if I'll recover. But, if you love something, let it go. A while ago I had written that "one of these days I'm just going to leave and never come back." And I just now became aware of its extreme relevance in this moment.

08 October 2010

I think Chadwick hates me more and more every day. Ah well, the feeling's mutual. I can't do what he wants me to do. He is trying to force me to play a way that I cannot play. It's not working, I'm doing everything wrong.

10 October 2010

Today I went to Uwajimaya with Lillian and Zara. We also went to this Asian dollar store in the Westlake Mall. I got a teapot and a mug without a handle. Right now I am lying on my zebra print rug drinking tea out of the mug. Best vibes ever. I also read some of *Zen Mind, Beginner's Mind*. It's so good; it makes everything so simple and clear and real and wise. And true. It makes a lot of sense to me.

11 October 2010

It's like we're searching for our true nature our whole lives, and all these things get in the way. Like consciousness, awareness, the ceaseless chattering of our tiny minds, and the feelings we have about particular things.

I wish I could tell you all the things in my head.

12 October 2010

I'm sick of seeing people's bodies. Everything I think is negative. I am tired, I am dreading practice. I hate today, everyone's annoying the shit out of me. I might go back and sleep. I have so many zits. I think I'm supposed to start my period soon, that may be why I am in a bad mood. I don't want to talk to anyone. Everything requires so much effort and I can't do it.

13 October 2010

I started my period today, holy shit. I meditated yesterday and today. I think it makes me feel better. I think my mind likes it. I'm not gonna worry about doing it but I'm going to try to do it whenever I'm in the room alone, which actually happens frequently. I feel so much better today though, it's ridiculous how much my period gets to me.

I just finished watching *The Motorcycle Diaries*, and it made me feel sad because I don't understand how privileged I am and how much stuff I have, when so many people are starving or have horrible diseases. I dunno, it was kind of depressing but inspirational as well, because the things they said were poetic and their relationships were real and imperfect and everything had meaning and struggle and hardships. Life.

It makes me excited to go to a real college and have adventures and not have to worry about running every day. I dunno. I don't think I'm going to come back here next year…

Tonight I also dyed a bit more of my hair, hung out with Tabby while finishing my Animal Biology assignment, and hung out with Lillian for a bit. Eugenia is in my Animal Biology class, so that's nice. It's been interesting so far.

Tomorrow we have a home game which meant that today practice was easy, which was the best thing ever. I am so excited for soccer season to be over.

I want to start watching more movies. I want to start truly realizing what I have and enjoying it. Like, I have a fucking laptop! How crazy is that?! I have forgotten how great that is. How beautiful its soft, clear complexion feels when I caress it. I can take it anywhere.

14 October 2010

We won our game today, and I didn't play bad but I didn't play that amazing. After the game Chadwick told me that I need to do fitness on my own. Like, do sprints or something outside of practice. I don't know why. I wasn't slower than usual or anything. I honestly feel like he just wanted to say something rude to me, just wanted to get in my head and make me feel bad about myself.

Anyway, I'm not going to do more fitness. I'm already exhausted as it is. He's a fucking idiot, I wish he would die. I wouldn't feel bad if he did. Not even a little bit. I'm so excited to quit. That sounds awful but it's real true. I don't care about it at all.

17 October 2010

I'm at the library downtown. Checking out books about Kurt and Courtney. Figures.

We won our game in Montana. Chadwick got pissed at me because I wasn't running fast enough. Hate. I didn't play very much at all. He took me out of the game and tilted his stupid potato bird head and squinted his stupid beady eyes at me and sneered, "What's wrong? Why aren't you trying?" and I said, "I don't know, I just don't feel good." When in reality I *am* trying, I'm just exhausted chasing around the other midfielder like he wants me to, trying to defend her instead of focusing on myself playing well.

Not being able to play all-out or express my creativity while playing is such a motivation killer. I am not allowed to do anything other than chase around the other midfielder whenever she has the ball. And when she doesn't have the ball I still need to be as close to her as possible to try to get the ball from her when she does get it. I am at no moment encouraged to try to get the ball myself without thinking about her.

And even if I were to get the ball on my own, I would still probably just fuck it up because my body won't obey my mind's desires. I'm just so fucking exhausted, mentally and physically, that playing well or to my potential just isn't an option right now. It just won't fucking work and I can't explain it. It doesn't matter how hard I try, *it just won't fucking work.*

But, obviously I can't explain this to Chadwick because he cannot accept that as an answer. He has to know *exactly* what you are thinking, what you were thinking, and he wants a complete logical explanation of your reasoning for disobeying his orders. I can't give that to him.

You could tell he was so pissed, shaking his head, huffing and puffing, and I didn't play anymore after that. Bailee, who was on the bench at the time, muttered to me, "You have to learn how to manipulate him, you have to just invent something." I hate playing these mind games, it's useless. It's fucking abuse.

18 October 2010

Well, I had a meeting with Chadwickles today...HOLY FUCK. Fucktastic. He is seriously the biggest asshole I have ever known! How is this possible? He basically told me that if I don't get more consistent then he doesn't want me on the team. He said that I'm not competitive enough, and a ton of other random shit, just putting me down and blaming me for a lot of stuff.

I cried a little bit when talking to him. I just can't care about it to the extent that he wants me to. I just can't. The more he pushes and tries to pry into my mind, the more I resist. And I can't tell him that because he will just become furious and that is more painful to me than trying to tell him what he wants to hear. I'm so apathetic and it bothers me, but not enough for me to do anything about it, because I'm just like, "Oh well, whatever."

So basically, I am for sure quitting next year and I'm not sure what to do in place of it. I really hate soccer. More than anything. It's awful because I used to love soccer more than anything. It totally defined me for almost my whole life. It still does, in a way. And I was so fucking good at it, too.

Chadwick just destroyed any kind of love or passion for the game that I had, and I feel I had so much. He's so controlling and demanding and won't let us play how we want, and always nitpicking and interrogating and questioning and analyzing our every move and thought. There is no freedom to find your flow because every mistake is highly criticized, so that you start to fear making mistakes, and that leads you to make more mistakes. It's just a downward spiral of anxiety and depression. It's like, make one mistake and you're taken out of the game instantly so that you can't get a feel for the flow of the game, which you need in order to play better.

Add all that to having your schedule strictly controlled (like having to meet up with everyone to eat the pregame meal exactly four hours before you play, which fucks up my body's energy levels because by the time the game is about to start I'm really hungry again), or being interrogated constantly about why you have done certain insignificant things like not wearing the same running shoes as everyone else during weight room, or not wearing the long sleeve version of your jersey, or wearing the incorrect style of sweatpants, or not wearing a costume to Halloween practice.

It's just so fucking exhausting trying to avoid Chadwick's negative energy that is constantly aimed at full blast in my direction, in everyone's direction in reality, but I'm just super sensitive and feel it more than everyone else. It's as if Chadwick senses that it affects me more and because of that he tries even harder to break me down.

Right now I am in the old science building and it is so quiet. I am in some random hall in a chair that is comfortable. There are no people anywhere, it's the best ever. I have to go to practice in about two hours. Suck.

20 October 2010

I went to a coffee shop last night with Jean, Lillian, and Zara.

I got a lot done and it wasn't crowded. I have three friends not related to soccer.

Tomorrow we go to Canada for a game. I forgot to say that Chadwick told me that he was considering not taking me to Canada. Trying to threaten me. Good thing my mind is an apathetic limp rag of hatred that cannot respond to threats.

I'm still struggling with my perception of the relationship between myself and soccer, and if I'm a bad person for wanting to quit something that I've done my entire life and that has been the center of my life for so long. I'm worried because I don't know what I'm going to do with my life. And I hate Chadwick so much. You can't understand.

23 October 2010

Yesterday at our team meeting Cameron and Molly told me that they have confidence in me and that they know a little bit about my situation with Chadwick and that they know I can do well. I just feel so stupid and frustrated with myself. Actually, I don't even know what I feel.

I honestly think that I am the worst communicator in the world, and that no one understands what I'm feeling, and that I can't show emotion or that I care about people without feeling stupid, and that I feel stupid a lot of the time. And awkward, and it makes me not want to try really hard because I feel dumb when I try hard and it doesn't work out (which is always). Especially when people I admire or think are way better than me are there or watching. Like Cameron.

I worry that when I'm older I won't be able to get a job because I'll just fuck it up, and this type of situation will happen again, where I am trying as hard as I can but it's never good enough. Or else I'm a complete idiot and won't be able to figure it out because I'm stupid.

I am nervous about our game tonight. I didn't play in the game in Canada. And then, yesterday Chadwick and I had to have a little talk, and he asked me how I felt about not playing, and that shows that he plays these little mind games. Like, I played hard in practice, and then he doesn't play me at all in the game, and then asks me how I felt about it.

And before even going to Canada he tells me he thought about not taking me. He just does these stupid, subtle, negative things to see how I react, or to make me think about why he's doing it, and I hate it so fucking much. He is such a fucking asshole. He will ask me to warm up, and then never put me in, so I'm just warming up for nothing. And I know that he isn't going to put me in when he asks me to warm up, so it's like what the fuck is the point?! It's so frustrating.

He has a secret agenda behind everything he says, every question he asks. I don't know what to do. Like, before this whole situation arose, I didn't even know I was doing that bad or not working hard. Obviously there were times, but it wasn't all the time, and I don't even think it was most of the time! I was just minding my own goddamn business and he has to ruin my life.

He plays God. Really. He has to influence everything, and know what everyone is thinking and why they think it, and then try to control them with that knowledge. At the same time, even when he is an asshole, he is not as much of an asshole to my teammates as he is to me. Like, there are other girls on the team that don't play that much, that sit on the bench just as much as I have been lately, and he doesn't do anything to them. He totally leaves them alone and, like, doesn't even interact with them that much. But with me it's different. He actively tries to terrorize me.

Sometimes I think about what troubles other people in the world have to deal with, and I just don't even get it. Like, how can something be bad in the way that my situation is? Mine is just a mind-fuck that doesn't even make sense. It would just make so much more sense to me if I was starving or poor or something. That would at least have a real reason or, I dunno, be real. Or be, like, something that a lot of people have to deal with and you could find common ground with others as support.

Right now it's just this strange misty world that isn't logical and no matter what I do, it's wrong. I am always being inter-rogated and having my words turned on me or blatantly misinterpreted, and I can't tell Chadwick the truth (about the fact that he is an asshole and I am playing worse because of him terrorizing me consistently over every single mistake I make) because he will just get really pissed off and deny any kind of responsibility and it will be worse. So I try to tell him what he wants to hear, but it's so hard! I feel like everyone else on the team is so easily able to manipulate Chadwick and tell him what he wants to hear, and I'm the only one that is really shitty at it. It sucks so bad.

The whole situation makes me feel like a bad person, or that what I do is never good enough, or that I'm lazy and apathetic. And that last part I am seriously thinking is part of my personality. I can't figure out if that means I am a terrible person. But if I were, so what? So what if I am lazy and I can't care about anything? I don't know if that matters. I don't know if anything matters. I just hate letting people down and I don't want them to believe in me because it makes it so much worse when I fail.

This is what I'm going to do: try hard even when I feel stupid. Ignore myself when I feel stupid or awkward. Try to say what I mean and be genuine.

God, I hate my life, I really do.

25 October 2010

I just finished my Animal Biology test. I thought it was hella easy. I can already tell today is going to be a good day. I haven't known what to say lately. Yesterday Syler texted me randomly, we are in love. Haha.

I haven't had any time to sit and write. I don't have practice or weights today, even though it's Monday. Yes! But I do have to watch our game that was filmed with my team at 4:30 p.m. We beat our ultimate rivals on their own turf, that's probably why Chadwick's giving us a day off. My parents come on Thursday because we have two home games in a row.

Things I thought about in Psych:

Soccer last year: I was still on the level of being liked and making friends rather than self- actualization, which would be playing well and to my potential? (Analyze with respect to Maslow's Hierarchy).

I'm afraid to do what I want because I might disappoint others?

ARE THESE FACTS ABOUT MYSELF? HOW WILL I EVER KNOW?

I was also thinking about how daydreaming of leaving this place is my coping mechanism to get through soccer when I hate it. Weird.

Eugenia was talking to me about problems with Sierra and Chadwick and her, like, drama that's going on right now, and I was thinking about how I think I feel the same as Sierra does. And it made me more confident in my decision to quit. Chadwick is a JACKASS!

I want to go to a coffee shop with my bike. Because I have a gift card. And a bike. Haha. I like my outfit today. I got coffee before Animal Bio. I have newly dyed hair (black and blue). I think I did fairly well on my Animal Bio test. No practice. All this means BEST DAY EVER. Okay I don't know what else!

Everything's my fault.

31 October 2010

I'm at a coffee shop. I bought a pumpkin spice latte with my gift card. Today's Sunday.

The past few days I've been sleeping at my parents' hotel. They left this morning early and dropped me off at my dorm at 7:30 a.m. We won both our games. I've been studying Psych. I just wrote, like, seven pages of my book. Or rather, transcribed. Good. I'm kinda hungry. And jittery.

I dunno what I'm doing tonight. I want to go trick or treating so badly. I got my laptop fixed; it was fucked up for a while so we took it to the Mac store. I also talked to my parents about not coming here next year. Legit.

Various emotions have been flitting across my soul today. They consist of a mixture of longing, nostalgia, excitement, worry, caffeine brain, coldness, hope, I don't know. Nothing else.

I bought tickets to the Gorillaz concert in Seattle!! Camila was going to come with me but she might not be able to go now. It's stressing me the fuck out. I was irritated today.

Zara and I got shwasted at the volleyball girls' Halloween party last night! No one on my team knows.

The role of madness in artistic genius is an interesting concept. It makes me pissed I'm not insane, because I'd be so much more creative if I were. But this conflicts with my past because those moments where I've felt truly insane were not pleasant moments.

02 November 2010

I'm going to go to Gorillaz, and I'm going to forget about everything. I'm gonna let it all go. I'm gonna be alone, I'm gonna be confused, I'm gonna be unsure. I'm gonna loathe myself. I'll be a shadow in the background of reality.

I dunno where I'm going. I hate this school so fucking much I wanna be hidden and safe with no obligations. It's too hard, how does anyone do it? My whole life I've been unsatisfied, happiness on occasion, depression most others. I don't like anything and I'm unstable. My perception of myself doesn't align with my perception of reality.

05 November 2010

The second law of thermodynamics has ruined my life.

I went to the Gorillaz concert; it blew my mind. It symbolized how I feel about everything. How I have ever felt about anything in my entire life. It was the sum of my emotional distress and euphoria regarding my bane, worthless existence. I cried the whole time. I cried until there was nothing left. Catharsis? Cathartic. It was something I couldn't explain, still can't, really. It was a mind thing, an emotional thing, not of language. It was enlightenment.

Now I'm in the university library. Nothing else cool happens. Same shit, different day. I loathe practice. When it's over I hide in my room and embrace the dim lights and the sound of the TV murmuring.

07 November 2010

Yesterday we won our game 4-1 and I scored once, and got a yellow card because I got in a fight, sort of, with another girl. It was kind of awesome.

Right now I'm in a secret Starbucks downtown with Zara. It's hidden and I found it once on the way to the public library downtown. We are going to study. I'm actually going to write my book, woo!

Last night I watched *Kill Bill Vol. 2* while studying. That movie is hella tight. I wish I could fight like that, then I wouldn't be scared to go places alone.

I am safe.

10 November 2010

I'm in a room in the university library with six armchairs. I'm wearing purple flowery tights and cut-off jean shorts and zombie-killing boots and a men's dress shirt and a necklace made of long brown feathers.

Yesterday Eli called me and it made my day. He's living in

LA with his aunt and has figured out what he wants to do with his life. I'm glad he knows what he wants, because I have no fuckin' clue what I want.

Time will tear these buildings down. I am a flimsy sliver in time's oak dresser.

11 November 2010

Self-medicated. The illusory enlightenment of an acid trip, the revolutionary awareness of unity. How it could be real if you weren't trapped in your own opinions and preferences. The creator, pen gliding on crisp notebook paper. The eccentricities of the brilliant and insane. Entropy in the universe is always increasing. The quest for freedom from ourselves, from our fucking burdensome brain chemistry.

You can't do what you want because you're trapped by inhibition, by social rules, by your brain's neuronal connections giving you phobias and fear.

Why does the city make me feel hopeless and desperate? I'm in a coffee shop downtown. A young man asked me where Urban Outfitters is, and I told him the correct location. It's 1:15 p.m.

We went to the aquarium at 10 this morning for Animal Bio. Eugenia drove. It was so interesting. My favorite were the sea horses. They are strange looking, like miniature mythical creatures in a haunting luminescence. They are tiny tinkering mechanisms with wheels for wings.

I can find letters to string together. I can choose my words in the way I sneak through forests, stepping lightly so no twigs break, brittle. I might like what I stand for. I might like the pureness of my soul if it weren't covered in mud and shit.

There's no purpose, but don't let this hinder you. There's always a thing and I always fail at realizing what it is.

Why do I feel the need to be completely independent when accomplishing a task? I asked this little bookstore downtown if they were hiring and they said not really, and that they are looking for people with 15+ years of experience. And then I felt really stupid for asking. I feel like things are so often complicated like this and it makes me feel lost and incompetent and like I'll never be qualified for anything.

I'm gonna write a fuckin' book, that's what I wanna do. And I always forget this, but it's something I would really like to do, and it seems like there is a possibility that I could earn money this way. Could I possibly want to be a writer? Could I have been ignoring this about myself for some reason? I've never really made up stories or anything before. I'd rather just write in my diary, or write poetry.

I know I don't want to be one of those business people in suits all the time. That sounds kind of shitty. I dunno. I'd like to be an eccentric artist. Fuck labels, though.

12 November 2010

I just took the biggest shit of my entire life. I got a decaf mocha before Animal Bio. We went over mitosis and meiosis again and I really get it now. Woo.

Today practice will be short because we have a game tomorrow. I'm in the university library waiting for 1:00 p.m. to come so I can go to the cafeteria when it isn't crowded. I want to write more. I want to watch more movies.

I dunno if I've ever said this (I probably have) but I sometimes really appreciate my existence, and I think about little characteristics of things and feel really excited about them. Or just get excited about things I'm going to do. And other times I don't at all. And when I drink caffeine I get excited and feel this particular way about everything.

I kind of feel this way right now, kind of high in a caffeine way, but I haven't had any caffeine so I dunno what the deal is. I want to read a good book. I still have to finish *Zen Mind, Beginner's Mind*. Okay bye.

13 November 2010

Quiet. One lamp on. Miles Davis. We won our game today. I started and played the whole game. Hmm. Dinner at Mariah, Kan, and Claire's apartment.

Back in our dorm Zara and I studied and watched *House*. I learned how to fishtail braid my hair, thanks YouTube. I also helped Tabby dye her hair.

Tomorrow is Sunday and studying. It might be sprinkling, the wind rustles the trees on occasion. I applied to Whole Foods Market last night online. Zara and I went to a party as well, but it was lame.

15 November 2010

Today's Monday. Just had an Animal Bio midterm, I think I did well. Prac today, blah, blah, blah. I also registered for winter classes. I am going to take Abnormal Psychology with Mila. I am in the university library. I was working on my child interview paper for Developmental Psychology. I don't think it will be hard.

Yesterday Jean and I went to the library downtown and worked on Geology. We are both taking that class and it's kind of boring but the professor is weird and funny so it's okay. I also got a book and a movie, which Zara and I watched last night and it was hella creepy. *Pi: Faith in Chaos.*

I feel like the adolescent transitions we've been talking about in my Developmental Psych class never applied to me. I never wanted to be like my peers, I was never stressed by changing from elementary to middle to high school. I was never a risk-taker, I knew what to do according to reason and logic and respect for others.

21 November 2010

We went to Texas for a game and we lost. Our season is over. Thank you god I don't have to deal with that anymore. We got drunk in the hotel that night after our game. I drank too much and made myself throw up before going to bed. We had to get up at four in the morning for our flight and I had a hangover (was I still drunk?) and was sick at the same time. Like, I had a cold, kind of.

I threw up on our second flight. I made it to the bathroom but it was awful regardless. My face was bright red and my hair greasy and stringy, and all my insides were outside. When I finally got back to my dorm I slept all day.

I am thinking things are impossible again. Like writing a book. I am not going to think about it anymore, I am going to forget everyone else and do my own thing. I'll write and be happy about it. Fuck poetry, fuck good writing. Fuck society's definition of good writing. I don't want to hate myself more than I already do. I don't know how I'm feeling right now.

23 November 2010

I've been in the airport for a few hours now, waiting for my flight home for Thanksgiving. Tabby is here, too. We rode the bus and then the light rail together to get here. It's been snowing hardcore here. Classes got cancelled for part of Monday and all of Tuesday and Wednesday.

Last night I hung out with Zara and her Asian friends that live on the second floor of our dorm. We played the board game *Clue* and took shots in their room and talked about boys. We played in the snow at, like, three in the morning in the back parking lot of our dorm. We drew pictures of dicks on the cars. There was a thick layer of snow on everything so it was good for drawing. I had a great time. And now I get to go home!

25 November 2010

Home. It's nice, I suppose. It's strange because I'm reminded of last year when I thought I was insane and started taking Zoloft. And in high school, when I read *The Bell Jar* and cried to Eli because autumn's bare trees in the twilight made me uneasy and aware of a liquid fear, tar-like and oozing. It's just fucking weird, like coming back to a once tragic crime scene and feeling time whirling around you. History is palpable, looming and mysterious and everything.

I'm watching *Criminal Minds* and texting Zara, who happens to be watching it, too. I played a lot of *Guitar Hero* today, with Lacy's Wii. I'm actually pretty good, it's weird. Today is Thanksgiving, dinner was delicious. I ate too much, naturally. I was also hella bored while everyone was playing Wii bowling. I felt useless. Being home makes me kind of depressed. I think subconsciously I go back to my depression when I'm in that old environment where nothing happens.

Also, I'm thinking that I want to study abroad in London for a year. I don't think Mom wants me to because she doesn't want to pay, but I want to help. I mean, if I get a job soon I could help.

I want to go to Thailand this summer if Sawyer and Lacy go there to teach English, which is what they've been talking about lately. I also bought concert tickets for White Lies! They are playing in Seattle and I am so fucking excited because I adore them. They know everything.

29 November 2010

Each period of my life has been characterized by a certain feeling. Right now the grayness of the cold reminds me of my past discomfort with insanity. There is a slight nervous anticipation of future events. Not a bad nervous, maybe even slightly good.

The usual solitary feelings are present. The feelings of Christmas and home and silence and gifts and snow and the shit-hole of Boise. Of going to see movies at the theatre and dying a little inside because that world is not my own. Of being isolated in the warm center of my hood and scarf while skiing. The endless thoughts, images, phrases, songs, running through my head while rushing down the mountain through the white chill. Dreams of recklessly flying.

Not knowing if I'm good enough to work, to have a job, to talk to people. To do anything. Can I write a book? Am I worthless? My thoughts are looming skyscrapers in a vast city of emotions and neurons, held together by a murky haze of possibilities and doubts. I'm my own worst enemy and I fear I will win.

Today was good. I'm back at school for finals before Christmas break. Jean and I presented our Geology stuff in class and it wasn't bad at all. Usually I am so nervous and my face gets red when I do presentations, but I don't think it was like that at all this time. Also the lights were dim so everyone could see our presentation screen, so they probably couldn't see if my face was red or not. God.

I also read my book during everyone else's presentations so I wasn't bored. I am not stressed at all this week, even though it's finals soon. I wrote my Animal Bio paper and studied a little for the quiz. It shouldn't be a big deal at all. Then I have to write my Psych paper, but that isn't due till Tuesday so I have some time.

I also meditated today – zazen. The first time in a real long time. I want to do it more but I just never do for some reason. It kind of annoys me that I put it off.

We had a team meeting for soccer. Chadwick told us that he cut Hope and Mari from the team, isn't that fucking crazy?! They didn't play very much anyway, but still. He never cuts people. We have our individual meetings in January. I am very much dreading it. I don't know what to expect. I don't know when to tell them I'm quitting.

05 December 2010

I think I like being high in my room. Writing is hard and I am afraid my speech is incoherent. I feel like when I say things people do not know what I'm saying and they look at me funny.

This is not a dark world, I am not going to remember writing this sentence after I write it. But anyway, I ate a little less than 1/4 of a mota brownie, went to the cafeteria and felt a little high there. I wrote a lot of my Psych paper, which is good.

My sense of time is completely out of whack. It's only been a couple hours since I ate it, but I feel like that was sooo long ago and I don't think it's been that long. It's hard to beat emotion with logic, and I have to be in that battle when I'm high and twitchy. I still have so much brownie left. I guess it'll just have to save.

~~I feel like when I say~~ I forgot where that was going...I'm really self-conscious around people when I'm highhhh as a frackin' kite. I hope these feelings are genuine. I'm trying to be earnest when I'm high, not fucked up. I don't want to be anything but real to you.

Listen to "Useless" and "High Noon" by Kruder and Dorfmeister. Sometimes it feels like things are slowing. Mainly I'm just sleeping. Those two thoughts are connected. There's a connection, that's why I put them in those words, in that specific format.

07 December 2010

I'm in the airport waiting for my flight to Boise. Home!

A shit-ton has happened. Last Friday there was a Christmas celebration on campus that a ton of people go to because there's free food and decorations. Zara, her Asian friends, and I got drunk before going.

After that Zara and I went to the junior soccer guys' house and drank more. We found mota brownies downstairs and I ate some because I didn't think they actually had mota in them…oops. Well, I guess I kind of thought they probably did. I don't know, haha.

Zara spit a bite out because she thought it tasted gross, so she never got high. I, on the other hand, did. I got *extremely* high, and I was freaking out but it was fine because Jack, who is this tall guy on the guys' team that plays goalie and that I had never really talked to before this, calmed me down and told me that he loved me and that I had to have faith in other people. I dunno exactly what he said because I can't quite remember, but his presence was comforting to me.

I felt like I was in one of those black and white photos of people from years ago, like before they had color photographs, at parties or just having fun. I always look at those and think about how much time has passed, and how my brain can't even comprehend exactly how long ago that must have been.

I look at these people and I wish I were them, all of them, because they look so genuine and happy and important. Like historical figures immortalized by the snap of a button and a little white flash. I felt like I belonged in that house, with the stumbling drunks and the Christmas lights and the music.

Mila, Trevor, Zara, and I stood in a circle and held hands, and Mila took pictures of Trevor and I holding hands so that it looked like we were dating or something. It sucks because I can't *really* hold his hand, even though I want to a lot of the time. We are kind of siblings because we have the same mind, a little bit. But anyway, it's okay because I felt like I was meant to be there, and it was a comforting feeling. I felt immortal in the pictures Mila took. I felt like things were okay.

Then on Sunday Tabby and I got mota brownies in Fremont,

and I ate some later that night. I watched *Spirited Away*, too, and it was so fucking cool. Those kinds of movies are perfect to watch high. Last night I got high again and watched *Howl's Moving Castle*, but I was just pissed, kind of, because I have the version where the voices are dubbed in English, and I wanted to watch it in Japanese with English subtitles.

My eyes got super dry and it sucked. I still have some of the brownie left but I don't want to eat it yet. It's in my bag right now.

I took all my finals so I'm officially done with autumn quarter! I'm excited to start winter quarter, particularly for my creative writing class.

I have been feeling relaxed lately. Like, for a while I was really worried about my future, about getting a job here and making money. But now I just don't care. Like, I don't freak out about spending money. I just bought a coffee from Starbucks with my own money, and I took the bus today and yesterday without a free bus pass from the student union building, and I took the light rail today with my own money.

I know that's not, like, big spending or anything, but still. I would do whatever possible to not hand over my cash. Now I just don't even give a shit. I'm not worried about what I'm going to do in the future, either. I'm just going to let whatever happens, happen, I suppose. Ugh, it's annoying to think about; maybe that's why I've stopped thinking intensely about it.

13 December 2010

So much time I have spent dreaming of Christmas break, and now it's finally here. No soccer, no school. Yesterday we got our Christmas tree.

Sawyer and Lacy are here. I am going to go to Ketchum with them for a couple days and hang out in the coffee shop Lacy works at. And sleep in their cabin in the snow.

Right now I am alone in my house, listening to Grizzly Bear and drinking decaf coffee I made. I started reading this book called *Naked Lunch*, which is about junkies, I guess. I think William S. Burroughs wrote it when he was shooting up heroin. I don't know. I need total silence when I read it because it's hard to understand. I like to read it out loud actually, in an apocalyptic tone, prescient of anxiety and death. It does scare me.

I've been transcribing my diaries onto my laptop for my book. I don't know what I want to call it. Sometimes I like it a lot, and then other times I want to smash my laptop over my own head for the sake of my limited vocabulary.

It's beautiful to hate yourself.

I'm excited for next quarter's classes. Especially Abnormal Psych and Creative Writing. I think the writing one will help me figure out the book I am currently writing. This one. Here, now.

18 December 2010

Back from Ketchum. We drank absinthe, played the card game *UNO* and Backgammon, built fires, peed outside, went to the thrift shop, roasted hot dogs, went to the hot springs and Lacy's coffee shop, woke up freezing cold, went to this other coffee shop called Iconoclast. It was fun, but I am glad to be home because we have electricity here, and therefore, a heater.

22 December 2010

I have been depressed and unsure of myself. I keep feeling like I have no self-confidence and I will be shitty at whatever I try to do. I felt like that today, but it's kind of gone because I applied to two jobs in Seattle online, and Mom and I looked up stuff about studying abroad. I think it'll work!

Mom and I watched *Eclipse* last night, the third *Twilight* movie, and it was the stupidest shit I have ever had to sit through. Honestly. The characters have no personalities! How do so many people buy into that bullshit? What has happened to society?*

I've been writing a ton of my book. It's going okay, I suppose. I keep thinking that I'll never get it published because so many people will have submitted better books. There are so many people in the world that I will never have an original idea. Isn't that depressing?

[*Ana: Society and its popular culture has always been super lame. The good shit is hidden. –J.]

27 December 2010

Things have gotten so much better. Christmas was perfect. I got a Polaroid camera! Yesterday we went skiing, it was fine. Today Sawyer and I went to a coffee shop and Davis met us there because he's obsessed with me. Then we went to a book store and I bought a book by Franz Kafka – *The Meta-morphosis*.

I ran today and on Christmas Eve and the day before. I'm eating better, a conscious decision. I'm becoming more comfortable with my decision to transfer to Boise State University and try to study abroad through their program. I think it'll be okay. That is all.

31 December 2010

Sawyer and Lacy finally bought their plane tickets to Thailand. I am TOTES going to visit over the summer. I already have enough money for a plane ticket, and I want to get a job during school. Hopefully it'll work, I wanna visit so fracking bad!

I go back to Seattle on the third. So soon. I'm excited but dreading soccer as well. Blah, blah, blah.

04 January 2011

Back in Seattle. At six tonight I have Creative Writing. Excited and nervous!

Yesterday I was anxious and it sucked. Kan made me nervous for soccer and I felt stupid. Like my winter break/whole life was/is boring. I felt really alone and like no one loved me. For no reason. God, I hate when this shit happens to me. Feelings are such bullshit, everything I feel is so irrational. Listen to the song "Welcome to the World of the Plastic Beach" by Gorillaz.

06 January 2011

Today I was worried and anxious about soccer and life. I got all ready to go downtown, and on the way to get a bus pass I saw Kan and Keith Henda, a philosophy professor that she meets with, talking in the student union building, so I sat with them for a while. I felt awkward. And sad because I can't talk to people.

Henda is friends with some of the older girls on the soccer team. I'm not really sure how they became friends, but he is cool and intelligent and maybe wise. Kan recently befriended him and he is kind of a mentor for her now. But he isn't mine so I can't confide in him. He's friends with everyone and I need someone to be only mine and I'll never have anyone.

I'm convinced I'm worthless and I'll never find a job. I want to be a part of all this, but I never will because I'm too terrified to ask if people are hiring and I can't ask for help from someone that could probably give me help. Like adults.

I want to be creative. I want it so bad and I don't think I am and it's all I want. I want to create something new. Something revolutionary. In my writing class I don't always feel incompetent, but I do when I hate my vocabulary, and that is often. I think I like that class because I feel like it'll help. I really think I'll learn a lot and things will be structured and I'll be able to organize my book now.

I wish I was fucking James Bond. I mean, I wish I was him, not that I was having sex with him. I guess having sex with him wouldn't be that bad either haha, depending on which Bond.

I wish I was really good at something, like drawing or something. I'm worried, I'm not worried. I always think that people just don't get it, get me, but sometimes I wonder if they actually do and I'm just a fucking idiot and can't accept them and that I *am* what I hate and am prejudiced about in other people. My brain is so fucked, I'm so fucked.

07 January 2011

I am drunk. I secretly want my Learning and Cognition teacher. I wish someone would love me, fully and unconditionally. I am at the junior guys' house. It's a party, mainly soccer people. I need to write. I probs won't remember this. No, I will.

I have real talks with Eugenia, and I feel AWFUL because I'm going to quit the team. I feel like I should tell her and my other teammates, but I keep it inside. I dunno what soccer means anymore. Chadwick's ruined it for me, but there's still this residual feeling that somehow I'm wrong and that I should figure myself out and be better than I am. Rise above myself. IT'S NOT FAIR how can I do this? I don't know what's going on.

Somebody's like me. There's someone that knows and I'll never find him. Do I want to fail because it's easy? Do I secretly enjoy feeling awful because people end up pitying me? And then I feel important because I have attention?

Flow, emotions, flow. I'm doing everything wrong! How will I know if I'm doing it wrong? I want to tell them and I can't tell them. Why can't I have the drunken mindset always? Why can't I always be confident? Why can't I know who I am and what I'm doing? Why can't I care? Why do I hate myself?

I hate when people love me because I can't love myself. And I love when they love me because I feel important. I want to love myself and I can't. Eugenia says it's about other people, it's not about me. When you have this mindset it makes it better. It works. I think of balance. I dunno if Eugenia thinks of balance, but I do. It makes sense.

Why can't I do the right thing? Why can't I feel the right thing? I'm quitting. I'm giving up. And I feel awful. I feel terrible.

I fear I'll never be a part of something this intense. This bonding. I fear I'll never see you again and you are important.

I have never had friends before that cared so fuc`
or at least that I felt cared, even when I failed or
or couldn't handle Chadwick. I'm so thankful a!
don't really deserve you but I try to pretend that
social anxiety prevents me from hanging out w`
and I feel left out, but I know it's dumb because I know they
would welcome me if I wanted to hang out.

Things are changing. I'm not the same as I've always been
and it's freaking me out. It's like I don't believe it's actually
happening. I don't believe that you exist. It's too good to be
true that you are real and you accept me and that you'll take
care of me when I'm crazy and I don't know what to do and I
hate myself.

I'm too sensitive, everything really affects me. I'm learning
that people care about me, and it's weird and difficult and
cool.

Listen to the song "Tarantula" by Smashing Pumpkins. He's
singing to me, only me. No one else.

09 January 2011

I got drunk on Friday night at the Green House. That's what
the guys have started calling their house. Because it's green.
Creative, I know. I wrote that entry on the 7th there. I cried to
Mila and Eugenia and told them I'm not coming back. It felt
better to say it.

We had our soccer banquet that night and I just kept feeling
terrible that I'm leaving these beautiful people, my teammates. These people love me, accept me, and I'm leaving
them and Seattle for fucking Boise State University.

Sometimes I think about being with people, and how they are

or that moment. They are entirely mine, no one else's. it's only like that if they are attentive, if their mind is in the moment and real. If they are not daydreaming about someone else, if they are not texting or Facebooking or thinking of something they think is more important.

I am going to meet with Henda alone. I'm terrified.

11 January 2011

Today was our first testing for winter workouts. We had to get up early and do sprints. It was all right, I guess. I felt hella slow, but I wasn't the slowest. Kan got the slowest time on the last sprint. Muahaha.

Also, we had our groups of six, which are practices for the separate positions, so my group of six was just the midfielders. It was okay. I am reinforced in my decision to quit. I dread the early morning workouts in the gym. I just don't wanna go, and I get nervous because I feel like if I don't get a good time when we do sprints, or at least keep up with everyone, then Chadwick is going to be pissed and we'll have to have a meeting so he can terrorize me.

Fear isn't good motivation for me. I suppose it motivates me, but not in a good way. It just makes me angry after a while and I want to rebel and not do anything. I'm not motivated to do well, I'm motivated to avoid Chadwick. It's all psychology. God. I am nervous for Friday, the first official morning workout. It's my birthday as well.

I had my writing class today and we got into small groups and shared our assignments on voice, and I really liked mine. I thought it was way better than the people in my group. I think I'm confident about writing! But then I scare myself when I say I'm good at it or better than other people because I think of how people that are like that – super confident – are, like, intimidating. Like Kan sometimes.

I don't want to be one of those people because it's like I'm betraying my real, genuine self. I feel like it's not me to be like that. But maybe I should be like that. Maybe that's what's wrong with me. Maybe if I became cocky or just more confident (even if it's not an accurate portrayal of my true abilities) I'll do better in life. I want the truth though, but maybe my mind determines the truth by lying to itself. If I lie about my abilities to myself so that I think I'm better than I really am, maybe I'll actually become that good. It's kind of a catch-22, a paradox.

People keep saying they love me, and I dunno what that means. I think it's sincere, but I dunno how to react when they say this. Rationally, I'm grateful. Emotionally, I'm so fucking sad and I feel like something's wrong but I can't put my finger on it. The thing is, nothing's really wrong, it's my fucking lack of serotonin. Or some shit.

Also, I wrote Sierra on my team a letter, because she has depression and anxiety stuff too, and has been having a hard time lately. I do think that our minds are similar and I needed to talk to someone, so I wrote her this:

Sierra:

I'm writing this because I think you understand. I don't want you to think that I'm trying to make your problems disappear – because I know I can't – and I don't expect you to feel like everything's perfect after you're done reading this. I think it's actually for my own mental health.

I just want to tell someone everything, I guess, without them judging me or thinking that I'm going to hurt myself or do something bad, because I'm not. Oh, I guess I do hope this makes you feel better! It's just not my main reason for writing to you. And I kind of hate myself for not being able to just talk to you, or talk to anyone for that matter, but it's easier this way, I guess.

Random random random things: I do hate myself a lot of the time, for no reason. And I get jealous of you and everyone at the Brick, because you guys are so close, and real, and have real lives and relationships. I want that so bad. And I probably have it, I just don't see it.

That night when we were all drunk and I said I wanted to be you. I'm sorry if it upset you. I think it's partly true. Especially last year. You are so fucking good at soccer Sierra, and it's all I wanted last year. I wanted to die so many times last year because I couldn't do anything right. And I really feel like I failed everyone, and I dunno why. Because I don't know if I actually did, but it felt like it. And it still does.

Kan, Mila, and Eugenia are the only ones who know this: I'm not coming back next year. I dunno how I'm going to tell everyone, because I love them, and you, so much. I hate saying that I love people because I don't even know what that means, and it feels fake when it comes out of my mouth. But I feel like a failure. A big fat fucking fail = college soccer for me.

I always think about Cameron. Because she's perfect, at everything. I would give anything to be her. I know that's a stupid thing to say because she probably has shit to deal with too, but I dunno. If I could even just be, like, good friends with her. That might be enough. Every time I see her though I am reminded of how shitty I am at things…life. And I feel like I disappointed her…and everyone.

God, I wish I could be a million different people. I feel like

I'm doing it all wrong. Like I'm not appreciating the things I should be. And there's nothing anyone can do about it. Like, everyone can tell me that they love me, and that I'm not a failure, and that I'm a good person, or whatever. But it doesn't change the way I feel about myself.

I try to think about myself the way I think about Cameron. I try to admire myself the same way I admire her. And it's so fucking hard. When I'm drunk it's easier. I write things down when I'm drunk and it's good, and I try to create that same feeling when I read it sober. It kind of helps.

I feel stupid writing this to you. I feel weak kind of, like I should just get over myself and be the best I can be. And that makes it even worse. I know you are really close with Henda, and tomorrow I am meeting with him, because he found out that my mind is fucked through Eugenia and Mila. But I feel stupid talking to him too, because he's everyone else's. He's not mine, he's yours. And I'm awkward, and all I want is to be genuine, but it sounds tense and awkward when I speak.

I don't know what I'm doing. I really have no fucking clue. Sometimes I have the greatest days ever, and everything works out and I'm happy. And other days I just hate myself so much and I wish I could be anyone else. I dunno how I'm supposed to feel. Are we all supposed to be perfectly happy and successful? Or is it okay to be self-destructive and melancholy?

I think I feel better writing this all out...probably because I'm going to give it to you and not hide it away. Oh, and don't feel like you have to write me back or anything.

Everyone looks happy all the time, and I don't like them. Like, I want to kill most of the girls on my floor in the dorms because they don't get it. I dunno what "it" is, but I know that

47

they don't get "it." I think you will, but if not it's okay. I'll just pretend that you do. My brain is too tired to think anymore. I'm sorry if any of this upset you. I really hope it didn't…

–Ana

15 January 2011

Yesterday I went to a party at Caleb's house and got super shwasted for my birthday. It was so fun! Zara made everyone sing to me and she lit candles and put them in Reese's cups. I could not even believe it. Ronan and Calvin bought me 99 proof alcohol! It's hella strong and I think it actually tastes good. They didn't make me pay because it was my birthday. I wrestled with Max, took pics with Mila, and picked out songs for Caleb to make me a mixed tape with. We also had our first official morning workout. It sucked but it wasn't hell.

Today Tabby, Zara, and I went downtown. Tabby bought me a Kurt Cobain picture at Pike's and a Hello Kitty magnet kit at a bookstore. I also dropped my movies off at the library and picked up a couple others I had on hold. I was in a bad mood though, because I wore horrible shoes for the rain and I was freezing the whole time. And, I dunno, just general feelings of pointlessness and futility that I always get. It was okay though.

23 January 2011

I am sick and we have a testing workout tomorrow and I don't want to go. Today's Sunday.

The White Lies concert was yesterday and it was beautiful. I was left feeling sad and left out because I wish I could be a part of that intense beauty, but I'm not. So many other people know the lyrics and love them too, and I don't want them to because I want them to be only mine.

Sawyer, Lacy, Zara, and one of Sawyer's friends went as well. Lacy was really drunk and tried to tell everyone it was my birthday, haha. We went to IHOP afterwards and I got chocolate chip pancakes. Fucking great.

Tomorrow Sawyer and Lacy leave for Thailand! They are going to teach English there and I want to visit them so bad.

P.S. I don't like my Creative Writing prof anymore because she doesn't get it. At all. She's says I'm too abstract. But I like the strange lighting of abstractness.

25 January 2011

I am excited for this day to be over. Morning workout, group of six, three hours of Creative Writing. Bleh. I went to Safeway to return stamps that I bought there, and they won't take them back. I guess that is a thing, not being able to return stamps. I didn't know because I'm stupid. So I wasted a bus fare for nothing.

Kan won't text me back and I need her ID card to print stuff at the library before my class in two hours. And I still have to buy treats for class. And I don't even want to go to class! Because it's three hours long and awkward because we sit at a huge square table and just stare at each other the whole time.

My fucking laptop is being an asshole to me. I have never been rude to it and it pulls this bullshit where it won't connect to the internet for no apparent reason. And I have a million zits and they won't go AWAY!!! Ugh, I am in the worst mood, I hate everyone. Okay bye, fuck my life.

In Starbucks. Thursday. We had weights this morning and it was all right. Morning workout tomorrow, Chadwick said he wasn't going to be there and I'm sooo happy! We have testing and I'm totes not excited. Last year I went on runs when we didn't have morning workout and this year I haven't, and I think this year I'm doing worse. It's weird. I think I'm doing fine with the upper body stuff, though. I dunno.

Recently I told Kan that she makes me anxious and that she's judgmental, and yesterday she texted me saying sorry. It was…I dunno. I don't want to make her feel bad, but I don't really think she can just not be judgmental anymore. That's just the way she is.

Sawyer and Lacy are in Thailand. I haven't heard from them but I think Mom has. Sawyer put Red Grundo, the little red stuffed animal thing we hide in each other's stuff, in my teapot and I found him yesterday while washing dishes. He surprised me, and I got him all wet on accident.

For Creative Writing I have to write a personal essay, and I'm going to write it about soccer here and how shitty it is, and how I thought I'd never quit college soccer because I feel like that makes me a failure, and how I'm about to quit anyway. I hope it turns out well.

31 January 2011

Tomorrow will be the worst day of the week because I have morning workout, my group of six, and my three-hour writing class. I totally thought I would love that class, but I don't. It's kind of boring. We had to write a personal essay, and I wrote mine about Chadwick and how he ruined my soccer life. I don't know if it is good or how my professor wanted it written, but it's the truth. It's not very story-like; I feel like it's more journal-like.

I think after tomorrow this week will actually be good. I decided that Tuesdays are the only days that are truly awful. All the rest kind of suck but it's not as bad as it could be.

I've been reading *The Fountainhead* by Ayn Rand and I really like it.

Yesterday Kan and I studied at the donut place by her work, then visited her work where we stole a million cupcakes and then watched *The Girl Who Played With Fire*, which was hella tite! I really liked it. Kan works at this small movie theatre and gets to watch movies and eat all the snacks they sell for free.

03 February 2011

I'm at the library downtown, sheltered by huge glass windows and monstrous buildings outside them. Kurt was in my dream last night. I put my arm around his neck and told him he was mine. I kissed his temple and left bluish lipstick. I woke up without him.

05 February 2011

Last night I got drunk at the Green House. There weren't a million people there, just soccer people, a couple volleyball girls, I dunno. People I didn't know. I'm in love with Cameron.

Today was gray and lovely and the air was fresh and cold and crisp. I felt rushed, though. I woke up sweaty and groggy and had to rush to the cafeteria.

The new soccer recruits are here and we went out to dinner with the whole team. It just blows my mind because I used to be one of them and it was the worst. I don't want any of them to feel the way I did. It sucks not knowing any of your team-mates and being awkward and uncomfortable, and I know that's probably how they feel right now. It makes me sad that I'll never really get to know them because I'm leaving, and I just feel weird. Like sort of failure-ish but at the same time not. I just want to tell them, "Don't do it! You don't know what you're getting yourselves into! Chadwick is awful and he will ruin any love you have for the game."

Right now everyone is at the basketball game and I am in Kan's apartment by myself. I made coffee and I can feel the caffeine working its way into my system. I love the way writing looks on paper. I love the way the coffee shimmers and sparkles in the light of the lamp.

I think it's crazy how I am experienced. How I know what the freshmen will be going through, what awaits them on the other side. I am adjusted to living without my parents. I am adjusted to being in a huge city. I await many more experi-ences, but right now I know things. I know that for them it will be hard to adjust and to play well. I'm so glad I'm done with that first experience, I can't believe I'm done with it.

Tonight I'm getting drunk at the Brick and I am excited! Ronan on the guys' team commented on my Facebook wall, "You make me feel tingly and uncomfortable," and I thought that was the funniest thing ever! Like, what the fuck does that even mean? So I was like, "ha ha uhhh…Want to be my boyfriend?" I thought I was fucking hilarious. Probably because I am. Gah, I am excited.

06 February 2011

I had a dream last night that I was supposed to watch over this, like, insane boy that was the same age as me, and I fell in love with him. He was so crazy, but in a good way. And it's fucking weird because all I want is to escape with him. All I want is to be asleep forever and run around with him on missions, and make sure he takes his psychotropic drugs on time. He was a foot taller than me. Freckles, a manic look in his eyes. He suffered but I understood. He knew I didn't judge. He was vulnerable but strong. I dunno, it's fucking weird as shit. Please let me fall asleep to him. Please let him be there when I wake up and I know I'm still dreaming.

10 February 2011

Yesterday was bad, I hated myself the whole day. The only good thing was that Kan, Zara, Caleb, and I went to the self-serve frozen yogurt place that Mariah works at. So fucking good.

Today's Thursday. Mom sent me a package for Valentine's Day! It was great. We had weights today, but other than that I don't have to do anything so I'm going to go downtown. I am in the cafeteria right now waiting for breakfast to start. Lunch, actually. I meditated too, which I think will help me have a better day, because yesterday there was just too much shit going on in my head. Also, I think I just needed to get away from all the people and I couldn't. I hope no one talks to me today. Haha. But seriously.

Last weekend when the recruits were here we got drunk at the Brick. It was so much fun! I felt bad though, because I really liked them all, but I'll never get to know them because I'm not coming back next year when they will be freshmen. I feel like a traitor. I dunno, whatever. It sucks because they have no idea what they're getting into, like Chadwick's mind-fucking psychopathic behavior. Whatever, I don't want to think about it.

At one point during the party one of the new recruits got way too drunk and was sitting on the ground and rambling to Cameron, and she looked up at me because I was standing close by, and was like, "And your style!!" Basically she was saying she liked my outfits. And that made me happy because she had good style too, and I wasn't even wearing anything that crazy at that moment. I dunno. It just made me feel good about myself. Because you know that whatever people say when they're drunk is probably true. People always end up telling me their secrets when they're drunk, it's awesome. So I know I look cool to people that don't really know me.

Today I got an assignment to make an annotated bibliography for my Learning and Cognition class, and I am dreading it. We have to get five sources and write two substantial paragraphs about each source. Also, for Creative Writing we have to write a short story (five to seven pages, double spaced) and I don't like the one I've written. It's already too long and it doesn't really have a conflict/resolution thing. So I'm worried about that, but it's due by midnight on Saturday so I have a lot of time. I am just embarrassed about it, and I don't want anyone to read it because it's stupid. I dunno.

Yesterday I was overwhelmed and worried about those things, and I just couldn't function. Tuesday night I got drunk alone in my room and worked on my story, and that helped me get started, but I still don't love it, and I don't know what to make happen.

16 February 2011

Lately I've been too in love with Cameron and it hurts my

heart. I got high last night and the night before at the Brick with her, Kan, and Kendra. Zara was there last night and we slept on the couch.

I'm leaving it behind, how can I leave it behind? Cameron will never love me the way I want her to. I'm extremely melancholy right now. I just want to get high all the time and stare at her until I don't feel awkward. I wish I could be her friend. I wish I could be genuine and serious and she could confide in me. I wish she didn't think I was annoying. I feel like she does, I don't know why.

I miss Kan so much. We haven't been hanging out at all lately. I am jealous that she goes to the Brick all the time. I'm jealous that Kendra and Cameron are like bff's for life. I don't want to do anything. I just want them to take care of me while I suffer with longing and misery. I feel like there's something else but I don't know what it is.

When I'm around Cameron I feel stupid and annoying and uncomfortable. But I find myself still wanting to be where she is and doing what she's doing. I always look at her to see if she's noticing what I said or what I did. It's like I'm looking at her for approval or something. Do I like this feeling? Do I want her precisely because she makes me feel unimportant? I don't know.

I want her to comfort me when I hate myself. I want to lay in her bed and smell her pillows and blankets, because it's her, it's her smell. My heart is cracking. There are fault lines and pressure points all over it and it's just a dull ache. I don't think it will ever get better. Is this going to be forever?

In Psych today we learned about inappropriate affect, which is like having the wrong emotion for the situation you're in, and I seriously think I have that. Not all the time, just often.

It's weird and I think I dislike this about myself. Like, when bad things are happening I just feel like laughing. And when people are happy I can't be.

Yesterday in my writing class we had workshop groups for our short stories, and it sucked. Because I'm bad at writing stories. It's like I have all these images and feelings in my head, and it sounds really cool when I think about it, but I just can't put it on paper. When I do it's disorganized, and all my characters have the inappropriate affect thing. It sucks.

I can't stand the people in the cafeteria right now. I don't know if that is true, that just came out of my pen, I wasn't thinking. I feel like I'll be bad at everything I try. I know this isn't true, but I feel it, and it blows my mind how I do this to myself. I don't know how I feel anymore. Everything's just everywhere a lot of the time.

21 February 2011

Today's one of those days where I want to hide. I just don't like myself because when I was working in the gym yesterday I did the washing wrong and ruined a couple jerseys. Jim, the manager, confused me on the phone when he was telling me which machines to use, and then he emailed me all pissed because I dried some stuff that shouldn't have been dried, and it melted the numbers on the jerseys.

I've worked in the gym a few times for a couple of my team-mates. It's not much money but it's better than nothing. And all you do is sit around and check out equipment to people and do your homework.

But I just think that I will fail at everything! Because apparently I can't get something so simple as the washing correct. And I failed at soccer big fuckin' time, and I always get the wrong thing at the store when Mom tells me to get something. I just think I'm fucking dumb sometimes. I dunno. It's stupid and unnecessary.

I have to meet at six tonight with my poster project group for Learning and Cognition and I haven't even started what I'm supposed to do. And I don't want to. All I want to do is not exist. And not try anymore because everything is hard, or not enjoyable, or I fuck it up. At least we don't have class today.

Yesterday I went to bed at 7:45 p.m. The night before that there was a party at Caleb's house and it was so fun! I wore my short, tight, white, lacy, ruffled dress. And I grinded on Cameron. MUAHAHA! I told her I am in love with her. Oops. She was way too drunk to comprehend though, so that's good, I guess; she won't remember.

The night before that I got drunk at the Brick with Kendra and Zara and Sierra's good friend's boyfriend Nick. It was awesome. Nick pulled his pants up really high and strutted around and said, "I got it" in this ridiculous voice. It was hilarious.

OH! Kan got her hair cut! Like Emma Watson's. HELLA short! It's so cute, it looks really good. She is totally able to pull it off. I went with her and took pictures while the guy was cutting it, it was great. But the reason this is so crazy is because she had really long hair before and she was obsessed with it and was always like, "I love my hair so much, it's so pretty!" And, like, fawned over it. It was actually kind of annoying, haha.

Well, I don't know what else. I just want to be hidden today. And not talk to anyone. I think I'll ride my bike around Fremont.

Last night Kan and I slept at the Brick and I got bad vibes. We watched TV all night, and I don't like to do that.

Cameron's only happy when she's high. The rest of the time I think she hates me. I wish I knew her whole life story and that I could be her friend. I think she smokes mota to deal with her problems. I dunno, I dunno anything. I just get that vibe. I don't know if I want to go over to the Brick anymore. I just feel like we aren't even friends. We just watch TV. We don't talk, we don't hang out. I don't like it.

It hurts my heart because I want to know Cameron and I never will. I feel really annoying lately, it pisses me off. I hate myself when I'm awkward and not genuine and weak. I hate it so much, and I think that's what I feel like around Cameron. But when I don't feel that way around her it's the greatest feeling ever. I feel important, in a sense.

I noticed that in my usual day-to-day activities, I have this lurking and pervasive sense of entrapment and danger. I never feel safe. I always feel like bad things are going to happen unless I can somehow escape. It's the weirdest thing ever! Maybe it's just my anxiety. I feel like I worry about food and shelter and money all the time, and I don't need to at all. I'm scared that I'll be homeless and constantly cold and hungry and uncomfortable.

It's bad because I don't know how to ask people for help, and when I do ask them I feel stupid about it. I keep thinking that I'll only stop feeling this way if I can become entirely self-sufficient, or if I get a job. I don't think that will make the feeling go away, though, because I do have a job, in the gym. Sort of. Kan works there, she basically got me the job by showing me how to do everything and giving me a couple of her shifts. And then I took some of my team-mates' shifts, and then they put me on the schedule as an employee. So I'm making money! Even if it's not a shitload, I still have an income. And I still feel extremely uneasy about money.

I wish I had confidence and didn't always underestimate my abilities. Oh, I think that my confidence in my decision to leave is raised after realizing that I don't want to hang out at the Brick anymore because I feel stupid there. I'm kind of glad in a contradictory way. Last week I felt too melancholic and uneasy and I didn't want to leave but I knew I had to. This week I'm over it. I'm ready to go. Maybe what I'll miss most is the grayness and the city and the idea that Kurt and Courtney walked these streets.

27 February 2011

I worked in the gym today. Hella boring. Kan visited for a couple hours and it was better. We watched *The Hangover* at her apartment later and ate a ton of cookies and ice cream.

I was a bit sad today. My sadness floated around in wispy threads while I thought about leaving people I adore and admire.

We went to the purple party yesterday. It's to celebrate all the birthdays in February and everyone wears purple. It wasn't as fun as I thought it was going to be, just because it was so crowded and hot and sweaty.

Kan and I had a heart-to-heart talk while we were drunk at the purple party. She told me I saved her life multiple times last year, like during winter quarter when she was having a really hard time mentally. She said she'd do anything for me and that she loves me. It just blows my fucking mind that I have a best friend! And that it's not superficial bullshit like so many people these days, in this life.

I've never had something like this before, never. I've never gone this deep with a person. She said I'm important. She said people listen to me, people respect me. She said I look so confident, that I have my own style. She said she loves me. And she said I'm a really fucking good listener and that I've taught her to be a good listener. I think I actually am a good listener, and I don't judge people – she said that, too – that I see good in people.

God, I'm just fucking grateful for Kan; she is a good friend. We've been through so much, like we've been annoyed with each other and hurt each other, but we always resolved our problems, and I think that is so important and meaningful. Like, my past friendships that could have been meaningful ended probably because I gave them the silent treatment when they were assholes to me. If that ever happened with Kan she would make sure it was resolved. She would get past the silent treatment barrier, and that is why she is such a good friend, because she knows how I act and she cares enough to help me change if I'm hurting people. It's so weird.

She values me and I need that. I really think I need people to remind me that I'm valuable, because I so often don't value myself. I feel like I've written a lot in here about how she irritates me or makes me feel bad about myself, and I don't want to make it seem like she is a bad person, it's just that our personalities clash sometimes. And I get irritable pretty easily. She really is a beautiful person.

Lately I've been feeling anxious, like bad things are going to happen, and just worried about things that aren't that big of a deal. I always feel like I'm not doing the right thing and that I'm not going to be happy if I keep doing what I'm doing. I

feel like I should be wearing other people's clothes and
sleeping at other people's houses and going places unpre-
pared. But I get anxious when I'm not prepared – if I don't
have something to sleep in, or my face wash, or if I'm not
looking fashionable in something interesting from my own
wardrobe.

It's like this thin layer of unsettledness that I need to peel
away like a second skin, but I can't get my fingernails under
it. It's weird. I'm, like, OCD when things aren't planned
perfectly or prepared efficiently. I think I need to do more of
the aforementioned things so I can get over my anxiety about
them.

I get anxious about doing the workouts for soccer. I'm afraid
I won't do well…or something. I don't even know if that's
it! Jesus. But it does not even matter at all. FUCK the workouts. FUCK Chadwick. ESPECIALLY Chadwick. Fuck
Chadwick to the extreme. He traps me, I can't be myself
because he's so overbearing and snooping. It's fucking
annoying as shit.

28 February 2011

I forgot to tell you that on Friday I slept over at the Brick
with Kan and Kendra, regardless of bad vibes. We watched
The Last Exorcism, which was only good for a little bit when
it got scary. Right after that we watched *Dinner for
Schmucks*, which was okay, but the best part was when Allen
from *The Hangover* is laughing and trying to keep a straight
face and his face turns really red. Best part of the movie. I
went to bed before it ended.

Cameron was in Spokane, so I slept in her bed. I pretended I
was her. I listened to the passing of cars on the street, the

birds in the early morning when I woke to pee. I pretended I was good at everything…

I was thinking about how *The Fountainhead* is revolutionary. It makes so much fucking sense to me. Emotionally, logically. I know that there are people that don't get it, that have never thought of it, and it distresses me. I honestly think Kurt got it. I really think he'd have liked *The Fountainhead*. He felt everything, I swear he felt it. It's "quality." What else could it be?

I can never explain it. I can never explain what I mean but I know it when I see it, and *The Fountainhead* is it. And Kurt, and Buddhism, and nameless little things.

Quality I want you I want to touch you and sift through you and vomit you and fuck you and hold you and be you.

I thought about Grandma's old house today. I thought about the nostalgia that floods my memories of it. I thought of the round glass table in the basement with all the pictures of relatives on it under the glass cover, and the black swinging chairs, and the little black TV, and the cupboards filled with sticky notes and tape. I thought about the red-carpeted stairs and the huge black ants we always found.

I thought about Camila and Maddie and our secret spy missions and "PWIYBLSSL" and jumping on the waterbed. And climbing on the roof of the shed out back – the vibrant, lime colored moss in cold misty air, the height, the stealth. The swings, the bars we played on. The popsicles in the freezer if we were lucky. The worn, brown, velvet couch downstairs, the hot lava game, watching TV all the time because there was nothing else. Cartoon Network! Youth. Secret agents. Sliding down the stairs in our sleeping bags into a pile of blankets and pillows. How it was all mine, safe and secret and lovable and fun.

I miss it randomly sometimes. I'll be doing something unrelated and suddenly it attacks unrelentingly, and all I want is that sense of security and home and family.

02 March 2011

This is what I typed on my laptop after the purple party when I was still drunk:

"Mila said Trevor and I can have a playdate with cameras and it will be okay. Trevor and I can hang out alone and it will be okay. Zara said that Ezra said that he wants to be my friend really bad. He told me that I'm cold. I'm really happy about it because I want to be cold. My personality is cold. Fucking awesome. I am drunk Ana. Remember this…Kan said she'd do anything for me. Kan said I saved her life last year. I will miss her so fucking much how can I leave her?"

Today we had our first official spring season practice with the whole team and Chadwick. It was okay. It felt really long, and we had to do sprints. But I played well. I scored a lot of goals, it was weird.

Well, tomorrow's Thursday and I don't have to do anything! No weights or class! I have a shit ton of shit to do, though. Lately I've been nervous about the future. I always worry about jobs and such. It makes me so anxious and I know it's stupid but I can't help it.

I started my period today. I took a shit today. I skipped Core today. Cool.

05 March 2011

63

Yesterday after class and practice I went to the Brick with Kan and Zara and we drank. Kan and I smoked mota by ourselves upstairs. It was fun, but the whole time I was thinking about how jealous I am of Kendra because she is good friends with Cameron.

Every time I look at Cameron I just start hating myself. Ugh, it's the worst. It's so unhealthy. I hate that I do this to myself! I don't even know why I like her so much. Like, I'm not even into the stuff she and Kendra like. The music they like is fun to hear at parties, but it's not real or good quality. I'm not all into sports (like watching sports or sports other than soccer) and the things they wear and the TV shows they watch.

I think I like her only because she's good at everything and I want to be her. I know I can't be her so I will just love her. And I can't really do that, either. So it's just a stupid fucked up situation.

And Zara's been kind of clingy lately. Not really, just…I dunno. Like last night she kept trying to make me do stuff and I was like, "No, I just want to sit here," and she wouldn't leave me alone. She kept grabbing me or leaning on me, and I just wanted to not be touched. She violated my bubble. It was weird because she's never done that before.

And I feel like today she just pried a little too much, like asking what I'm thinking, and I don't know. I think something is on her mind that she wants to tell me, but she hasn't told me. She is acting differently and it's making me uncomfortable. I just feel this weird tension. God, do I over analyze or what?

Sawyer emailed me today from Thailand and I am eternally jealous of him and Lacy. He said they went hiking through the jungle and saw monkeys and elephants and have been having an awesome time. And they're going to teach English and get jobs. I am going to visit; it has to happen or I'll die. Seriously, I have to. Because I can't do this anymore. I can't live in Boise. I can't stay in Seattle because I'm quitting and I hate this school and I can't get a job.

I don't think I could stay in Seattle anyway. I've been here for almost two years and it's getting old. I NEVER would have thought I would say that. Because I've lived in Boise my whole life and I never thought I would get out. I never thought any place as cool as Seattle could ever get boring. But I think that because I lived in Boise for so long I can't stay anywhere for too long. I need change to stay alive. I dunno, it's weird.

I just want to explore. I want to find something. I don't know what it is, but I know that when I find it I will know it's important and real and what I need. That's it! I need something and I dunno what it is.*

[*Ana: It's astrology. It's Jung's ideas of archetypes and the collective unconscious. It's symbolism, myth, the idea that everything is connected, an intimate understanding of your own natal chart, theurgy involving Saturn, a balance between polarities, a master you deem worthy of enormous respect. –J.]

08 March 2011

Next week is finals and then spring break. I'm going with Tabby to California! She is from San Jose, so I will visit her for the first half of spring break, and then after that I'm going home.

15 March 2011

Many things have happened. Yesterday was the last day of real classes. It's almost spring break! I also took my Learning and Cognition final, which I think I did well on. Then Kan and I went to a coffee shop and did a shit ton of homework. We also talked and it was so good. She is my best friend.

We also talked to Henda, the philosophy professor, together and it took forever so we skipped our Core class. Did I ever say we have that class together? Hmm. Well that was a few days ago.

I sent Henda my personal essay about Chadwick and soccer, and he thought it was amazing. It made me so happy. I think I forgot to say that I did meet with him a while ago, and that it was all right even though I was so nervous I thought I would die. He talked the whole time about anxiety and depression and just random shit, and it made me feel way better. Today Kan and I are going to meet with him again, I think.

16 March 2011
THINGS I WANT:

quiet, warmth, the death of God, no bloated feeling, decisive-ness, perfect body, no more Chadwick, no more anxiety about running, healthy eating habits, to be published, to be the ink in this pen, to be surrounded by water, to know everything, to hurt this stupid girl that lives on my floor named Tana, to hurt others, long hair, no zits, to not be at this fucking Christian school, no fucking idiotic fools at this Christian school,

to have a guy I can boss around, to be able to talk to people, to go to Thailand, to go to Europe, to do what I feel, freedom, someone who can figure me out without effort on my part because I haven't figured myself out, to let the unconscious flow, to feel that I am in the right place, to feel safe, to see

Mom, to feel secure in a job, to not want to feel secure in a job, to not need anyone, to need someone, to never feel fear, to be suave and savvy,

people without religion, Buddhists, someone that fucking gets it, never to hear talk about Jesus again, intelligence, abstract thinking, piercings, tattoos, AYN RAND, revolution, genius, creativity, destruction, blood, needles, clear thinking, sanity, no fear of insanity, no trapped feelings, no boredom, always the caffeine mindset, hitting bottom, letting go, someone who understands these concepts, Camila, Syler, I want Syler, care-free, enlightenment, Sawyer, no Lacy all the time,

to write important things, to not be around people my age, to not live in Boise my whole life, to be original and irreplaceable, to understand the mind, to be a part of Gorillaz, to be Noodle because she is respected, to be part of something important, to be respected in the way the genius youngest child is

Topics for exploration:

unrecognized genius, distress at social humiliation, feeling stupid or ignorant or bad quality, negative emotions, being awkward around people you wish you could impress, no confidence = self-loathing, wishing you could take your own advice

18 March 2011

I'M DONE WITH FINALS! Fucking finally.

Last night there was a party at the Brick and it was the best EVER. The minute Kan and I walked in the door we were attacked by people that love us. And that's the feeling that

I'm always searching for. The feeling that you belong in a certain place at a certain time and that's where you are *supposed* to be. I love that feeling, it is so meaningful.

Eugenia kissed me on the lips. Mila said that Trevor is in love with me and that she is 100% willing to share him. I was like, "Noooo!" And then she pushed me into him and took a million pictures of us together. It was so much fun. I wore the leopard print miniskirt I have with the camouflage shirt with the skull on it that Sawyer gave me, and tall socks and boots. Hot.

Everyone was so happy and I just want to cry because we are not always like that and I feel bad. I wish everyone would like each other and say what they feel, but it never works like that. I wish I could be in that moment forever and not be anxious or depressed or self-conscious of what other people think. I just felt so safe there, and I can't fucking believe that so many people love me and enjoy my company. It blows my mind.

Ed gave me three shots of his 50% alcohol, and Trevor gave me a shot of his alcohol. I smoked mota with Kan and Cameron, and then later Trevor and I smoked. I guess that was a big deal because Cameron was really surprised and wanted to take a picture, but I didn't let her because I wanted it to be a secret mission. Trevor is crazy. I think maybe he never smokes so that was why it was a big deal.

Now I'm in the airport waiting for my flight to San Jose. That is where Tabby is from. I am going to visit her for a week or so before I go home. Spring break! She was here as well but her flight is an hour earlier than mine so she went to her gate already. I feel kind of anxious because her friends don't seem very welcoming. They told her I couldn't come to the party that they're going to tonight...but I don't think I would want to go anyway.

I think I am feeling kinda down. Probably because it's the end of the quarter and things are changing and I am reminded of how I don't know what I want with my life and I don't know what I'm doing. God, I wish there was a guy in my life to make things interesting.

I was thinking today that school is the only thing that I do in my life that is like a job. When school is over I am going to feel so purposeless. Because what do I want in life? Nothing. Well, not nothing. I think knowledge is what I want, or what I've been made to want somehow. If I'm not learning something new and expanding my mind, what's the point of living? God, I am so depressing! But seriously, I don't know what the fuck I'm doing and I feel like when school ends, like when I graduate or whatever, I'll be purposeless.

Purpose is so important to me, I don't know why. I think I have this fundamental desire to preserve everything. For example, my thoughts immortalized in this diary. I want to keep everything and remember everything, and if I can't keep it I want to recycle it or reuse it or sell it and get money out of it. I hate wasting things! So I want to keep my intelligence, flex it and use it and preserve it.

Random: I feel threatened by a lot of things: new people, new situations. But, at the same time I need change or I get extremely bored and start to feel like I'm trapped in a cage or a prison. That exact idea is from *Eternal Sunshine of the Spotless Mind*. In the movie Kate Winslet basically says that her boredom turns into feelings of entrapment and when I watched it I realized that is *exactly* how I feel all the time. That's me, I think that is me.

After I was done with most of my finals I went downtown and returned movies at the library and walked around Pike's and went to a coffee shop for a while. It was nice; alone, music, sunny. I swear everyone was looking at me. So many people made eye contact and smiled, or I just caught them looking at me. It made me feel good about myself. I love when people stare, it makes me feel powerful. It's like I'm saying, "Yes, I look awesome, fuck you for being normal."

This weird guy on the bus started talking to me as well, and I didn't want to talk to him. When he first came up to me he was just moving his body weirdly and trying to mess with me. I laughed, and he said I looked like someone to be messed with. Whatever that means. Okay, I'm going to go to my gate now.

19 March 2011

Tired, past midnight. At Tabby's house. Today we went to the mall and I bought a sweet Nirvana book and a book about psychotherapy and Buddhism.

The Nirvana book made me think about Kurt, obviously. I started wondering if I would like him if he weren't famous. If I just saw him walking down the street, or knew him before he was famous, would I like him? Would I? Or would I see him as just another stoner? Like Tabby's friends. I met them today and they smoke mota every day, and they just seemed so unimportant to me, like just a couple more people out of the millions that don't understand me.

I feel like they don't get it, they don't get how there is so much more to the bullshit surrounding us, and I don't feel safe when I'm with them. I don't want to feel that way about Kurt. Haha, okay, stupid. But I seriously think that he got it. I think he kneeeewwww about the feelings I get when I'm obsessed with someone and I feel so secure around them and like they are where it's at, where the world is at. They are the group I want to be a part of. He's what I think of when I feel these things.

So many people I see and I feel that they are useless, and I know that's a horrible thing to say because they aren't. It just feels like that to me because I can feel that they don't get it. It leaks from their pores, it's running down their skin and hiding in their hair. Like Tabby's parents. Her mom is so nice, but it's obvious she isn't happy, she never looks happy, and her dad is kind of mean...I just feel like they don't get it, they don't know.

They don't know! Howard Roark knows, Dominique knows. Ayn fucking Rand knows everything. It's revolution, it's soul. It's not the stupid shit on the radio, it's not the fake tan and the makeup and the falsity superficial conversations where everyone judges and everyone is dramatic. Like fucking *Jersey Shore*. I hate that show so much. They aren't real!

What it is is when we're drunk and when you can tell who the genuine people are, because they're real even when they're drunk. You can tell by the way they speak, you can just tell. I can group people into categories of who is it and who isn't it. I can't explain the standard characteristics of the category, the exact characteristics that each person would need to have to qualify for that category, because every person is different. You just know. It's so apparent, so startlingly noticeable.

I wish people would think about this shit. I swear to god just thinking about this makes me the definition I search for in everyone else. Wow...I'm fucking self-absorbed.

21 March 2011

Tomorrow Tabby and I are going to San Francisco! I am excited. I'm bringing all my cameras, except my digital because it ran out of battery.

We've done a lot already. We went to the mall all day and hung out with a couple of her friends, who smoked mota in their car. I don't think they are cool. We also saw *Gnomeo and Juliet* with Tabby's little sister, who I really like because she is hilarious. Today we went to the beach at Santa Cruz and then walked around downtown.

We are going to ride the train to San Francisco, and Tabby's friend Michelle is coming with us. I like her. Her cheeks are pierced. I'm glad she's coming because that will distract Tabby from annoying me the whole time, haha. She has been getting a bit annoying but it's not too bad. I guess I'm easily annoyed as well so maybe that's not saying much.

This is going to sound absolutely terrible, but Tabby's obesity disgusts me. Like, she eats so much and eats a shit ton of fast food and never exercises, and I feel like I'm getting fatter just hanging out with her. Isn't that awful? I'm a horrible person for saying that. I feel bad, but it's true. I feel fat because I haven't worked out. I am not sure if I've been eating that badly; I don't think so, but I feel bloated.

23 March 2011

I don't want anything to do with stupid rules about what is better and what is worse. About anything. About religion or what to major in. I don't care about society's labels, and I especially don't care about the people that depend on these rules and follow these rules and live in these rules. I hate it. I hate it so much. They're so blind, they don't think for them-selves, they don't know there is anything else. Ugggghhhh.

Home tomorrow morning, flight is at 9:40 a.m. I'm so excited, I can't wait to get out of here. I don't like who I am here. I am sad because of Kurt, jealous because people know more about him than me, mad because most of them don't get how he hated fame and was confused because it's all he wanted before. They don't get how he hated labels and hated society and how everyone picked apart his every word. I'm probably making this all up. I don't care.

I think Courtney Love (I'm watching a documentary about her right now) gives me strength. Because she makes me realize that I'm not fucked up at all, and anyway it's okay if you are fucked up. You're not a bad person for it. Also, I dunno what makes a person a bad person, because it's always perspective, everything is perspective! I dunno what I'm supposed to think anymore. Fuck.

25 March 2011

Today is my second day home. The other day Tabby and I took the train to San Francisco and walked around downtown. I wanted to go to the Golden Gate Bridge, or at least go somewhere in view of it, but we didn't get to. We got to go to Chinatown and walk around, so that was cool. I got so sick of hanging out with her though.

Today Mom and I talked to the Boise State University people about studying abroad, and I really think it's going to work out!

27 March 2011

It's Sunday and I am wondering if I will survive if I have to live here, at home. I hate all the people here; they are rednecks or religious, or both, and they don't understand the secret concepts of revolution, of thinking for oneself, of truth, of self-sufficiency without a god.

I need people to entertain me. I need Camila, I need Sawyer, I need Kan. I can't sit inside this house all day, that's what gets to me. But the thing is, there's nowhere else to go. It's too hot to go outside and I don't have any friends and I can't be around my parents all day.

I don't need to do anything. I can do whatever I feel. Fuck 'should' statements.

30 March 2011

In *The Fountainhead* there's a phrase that mentions how a person that worships another is himself deserving of worship or reverence. And this is it!! This is exactly it! It's beautiful to hate yourself. It's beautiful to worship others, look up to others, want to be others. It's this exact feeling that makes you an object of reverence for someone else.

I worship people that have worshipped others, that have felt so strongly. Kurt Cobain – brilliant and hated himself, yet I worship him. Me hating myself. I am important just like Kurt is important, simply because I feel so strongly. Oh my fucking god. This is why I love *The Fountainhead*. Ayn Rand knows everything, I swear.

01 April 2011

Back in Seattle for the last quarter of school. On my flight I had to sit next to this cowboy or something. He was nice, but seriously violated my space bubble (which, admittedly, is kind of large).

I had Social Psych this morning at eight. I think I like getting up early. I like my professor, I had her for General Psych. She's funny and nice and I think she might get it if I told her. I decided I love my schedule. I have so much time! And practices are at convenient times so that I don't ever have to rush.

I had Visual Arts yesterday and it was cool. It's two hours long, though. But we got out early so that was nice. Josie on my team gave me her Sunday shift in the gym for this quarter, so I'll have an income.

Yesterday we had practice and it was awful. The day before went well and I played well, but yesterday sucked. Definitely not the worst I've done, but shitty. I just started hating myself. A lot. I feel like I'm incompetent and that I will be incompetent at whatever I do. I can't fucking talk to people! Jesus Christ, I can't. Ugh I hate myself so much. I can't say what I feel and I really think I'm dumb because of it. Cameron is perfect and I feel so stupid around her and I don't want to feel stupid around people.

I watched a video yesterday of Kurt singing and he looked so unselfconscious and confident, and then I hated myself even more because I'm not him, and I don't have confidence like that in my element. Or whatever. Soccer. UGH.

02 April 2011

My head rings when I drink too much. I am hella drunk and texting Syler. In Mila's bathroom at the Brick. This moment is so short but hopefully I remember forever.

04 April 2011

It's Monday. Social Psych was hella interesting. One more class to go for today. I am dreading practice. We went to

Canada and I played all right, I think. Not amazing. For some reason I just hated myself so much. Not cool. And I dunno, it's stupid and it sucks but I like it. Sort of. Because it makes me special and important but I still hate it. Cameron influences it.

Cameron and Kendra are best friends and I'm stupid for being jealous because I have Kan and she's amazing. Kan needs me and I need her. I always wanted a best friend. I used to write about it a lot, I think. Then I never realized how special it is to have one. Do I take it for granted that I do?

Anyway, we tied and won our two games. I assisted Kendra on her goal in the second game.

On Saturday I went to the Brick with Kan, Zara, and Kendra, and I got wasted. I was the only one drinking, and I drank six shots and threw up. Zara took care of me. That's when I wrote that last entry.

Last night I had dreams about killing people. And living on the ocean and having killer whales jump everywhere around us. And going underwater and meeting people. Strange. I should meditate more; I haven't in forever. If I do it enough I might have lucid dreams and be able to control what I do. I would totally fly the whole time if I could control my dreams.

I wish I was like Kendra. She's so happy and energetic and everyone likes her instantly. She's really funny. She can talk and it's fine with her. No anxiety in that mind, just flowing excitement and optimism. But I'm not sure I would seriously want to be her. I wouldn't mind, I suppose.

05 April 2011

What I want: to be an artist, to make something people

admire and are inspired by, to not have a boring fucking job when I'm older, to not feel stupid, to know I'm beautiful and lovely and tragic and important. To be where it's at.

07 April 2011

I got real high at the Brick the other night with Anne, Kendra, and Kan. Anne is another freshman like Kendra but I don't know her that well. I didn't feel that high but I think I was because I smoked a lot. We made videos on Kendra's computer, and Anne and Kendra made *365 Things to Talk About with Anne and Kendra* to post on YouTube. It was so fucking funny I couldn't breathe.

Last night Zara and I watched *Eternal Sunshine of the Spotless Mind.* Yesterday I cut my wrist with a razor. Just to see how it would feel. It felt sexual. I think that might be weird. I liked it though, because I know I shouldn't do it, and that if anyone knew they would probably be concerned. It just felt good because it was like a decision, when I'm always so indecisive and incapacitated. This was like a commitment to a decision that I had made, and I followed through with it, and it was a secret thing that I did by myself. It made me feel kind of free and not anxious.

The other day Kan told me that even as a little kid she always knew that she was going to do something great for the world, and that something would be helping people. I wonder if everyone has that feeling that they are special and are going to do something great. Because I totally have that feeling, and I've had it since I was little, too. Except mine seems more egotistical. I feel like I'm just going to establish myself as someone with influence, whether that be good or bad. An artist, someone I feel is more important, feels more than others. When I cut myself yesterday I felt like that. I liked myself when I did that, I don't know why.

08 April 2011

Today's Friday. I had two classes, and then Kan and I drove to her house a few hours away with her Dad. I slept most of the way. We ate a bit there and then drove to the woods to participate in this silent retreat thing, which is where we are now. The high school she went to has a silent retreat every year, and it's just where you hang out and do whatever you want, but don't talk. I think it'll be so relaxing because talking is what makes me anxious.

In our cabin there are 12 beds, all stacked on each other in various parts of the room. It's fucking legit. It's just Kan and I in this cabin. It's not cold because we have electricity and heat! We ate dinner, introduced ourselves to the other people here, played games, and then one of the leaders read a story about a "rag man who took everyone's sorrows as his own." I liked it. Then we started our silence.

I feel bloated and gross because I ate a lot of sugar when I wasn't hungry. As usual. I want tomorrow to be a good food day.

It's nice here because we are in the woods and it smells like fresh pine. There are little waterfalls everywhere and a river. I'm so excited to just wander around and listen to nature and read. What a great way to spend the day. I have no obligation to do anything. Just be peaceful. I've never gone a whole day in silence before. I've felt weird lately and I can't figure out how I feel. Maybe I'll figure it out tomorrow.

09 April 2011

Today Kan and I woke up early to eat breakfast and then fell back asleep for a couple hours. We went on a run that was only, like, five minutes because there's nowhere to go really. Up the road and then to a meadow, a space so large and empty and welcoming. Especially if you're alone. After that we took showers and explored, and went our separate ways kind of.

I found a hammock in the mountains! I lay there and looked up at the trees and listened to the waterfall that was near. In Washington everything is green and the air is moist and cold and the sky is always gray. It's my favorite weather ever. I adore it; it shelters me and I always feel safe.

When we were at Kan's house I started to feel so nostalgic for childhood. Like the evenings when it was quiet and we'd run around outside playing as the sun fell into sleep. And summer, and camping. I'm fucking 20 years old. Jesus. I'm going to miss my friends from college. In other words, Zara and the people on the soccer teams. And Kan.

Kan knows I cut myself because she saw it. I knew she'd notice it. She showed me a cut on her shoulder and then pointed to mine. In the car on the way to the silent retreat she said she was worried about me. I don't know if I gave her reason to be worried.

I don't know how I feel about life anymore. Or how I feel about myself. I'm just tired. Tired of school, tired of talking to people and trying to pretend to be happy and bubbly and excited, tired of soccer. Tired of thinking. I dunno what I want, I dunno who I am, I dunno what I'm doing. I feel unhealthy. I feel car sick all the time, on the bus when I go downtown, in Kan's car.

I want to buy a blank notebook – a sketchbook, for painting

and drawing. I want to paint with watercolors. I want to paint with my blood.

The sun is peeking out right now, warm and bright. The life source. I need nature. I need silence. I need people. I like to be silent around people. I like to be silent with Kan. I really need to break the rules. I want to hit bottom. I want to fuck someone violently. I don't really like my body all the time, but sometimes I love it viciously and terribly. I can see how it could be beautiful to someone.

When I had that seizure over the summer, I remember that while running I couldn't see anything. I couldn't focus on anything, like when I get super hungry and feel faint and blurry. That's kind of how I've felt lately. Like running this morning with Kan: the ground was just everywhere.

Everyone has insecurities and doubts. You're fine. You're fucking fine. Pretend you're the shit, because you are. Fake it till you make it.

Silence, tired, everything is real and I am a part of it. I never want to leave. I want to always be silent in nature, I don't want to be a part of society anymore. Cool, slight breeze. Alone.

11 April 2011

Back in Seattle. Today I had a panic attack at practice and left early. Everyone was yelling at me to do different things on the field, and then getting frustrated with me when I couldn't do what one person wanted at the same time as what another person wanted. It sucked away all my energy. All I could hear were angry comments and voices yelling at me and I started to cry because I couldn't handle it, I couldn't do what everyone wanted. I couldn't be in 10 different places at once.

I was choking on my breath so I ran to the bathroom and just broke down. I was so angry with everyone for not realizing that at least half of my teammates and both coaches were screaming at me continuously. I was also angry with myself for getting frustrated, but also unable to get over that frustration of not being perfect, of not being able to overcome the negativity all around me. It felt like being sucked into an infinite black hole of despair and meaninglessness and failure. That is how soccer has always felt for me here, since day one, and today it all came crashing down.

Kan and Claire were there for me and helped me calm down, told me to breathe. Chadwick stormed into the bathroom and was an asshole and wouldn't leave me alone after I said I didn't want to talk about it. God, I hate him more than anything.

Condescending, a snarl: "Well, Ana, we don't think it's very good if you just give up," turning me into the perpetrator, the culprit, the one in the wrong. Me, yelling, "I'm not giving up, I'm just trying to breathe! I'll come back out if you just give me five minutes!"

He just stared at me like I was the biggest idiot he had ever seen, and cocked his head in that stupid fucking birdlike manner that I despise. He's fuming because he can't control me, and he won't leave. I want to stab his face, knock his head against cement and scream and scream and scream. I want to stick my thumbs in his eyes, pop them out of their sockets, feel warm red gushing. I want him to suffer. I want him to die.

Eventually Kan and Claire made him leave. Kan came back in alone, and we sat on the tiled floor of the showers and I cried and she listened. A while later Chadwick had to interrogate her about what I was feeling and why I had a panic attack. He has to get to the bottom of fucking everything. I hate it, he can't just let something happen, he has to analyze it to the very last thought of every person that witnessed the event.

I didn't go back to practice. When I left the locker room to have Claire drive me back to my dorm, Kan was standing outside after her interrogation, and I went to her and hugged her. We just stood there, me with my red, swollen, watery, crying face buried in her shoulder and her with an anxious expression and tousled hair. In that minute she was the only thing that existed; she was safety from Chadwick and self-hatred and frustration.

In that small moment I realized what love is. Not a sexual love, but a human love. A love made of tiny connections everywhere, of wavelengths and vibes adjusting to each other to form a fluctuating truth. Kan is love, being there for me when I hit bottom. That is what a best friend is supposed to do, and she did it.

That's never happened to me before. No one has ever been there for me during those moments where I can't stand myself and I can't stand the world. I've never had such a strong cable of understanding with another person, and that's all that matters in this life, connecting with another person to such depth. It's crazy because she knows when I'm experiencing those horrible moments, and no one else does. I'm so good at hiding what I really feel and not letting people in, but she can see right through it. We have the same mind and it's real and true, and I'm grateful. I don't think my human mind can grasp how meaningful she is, it's beyond me.

Anyway, I'm so drained right now. I'm alone in Capitol Hill at the coffee shop Bauhaus. Kan was here for, like, five seconds, but now she is meeting with Henda somewhere near here. I've been painting with watercolors in a sketchbook I got at a bookstore when I was at Kan's house. We went there after the silent retreat and we visited her sister at work and saw her awesome apartment in Portland.

We rode the train back to Seattle this morning. It's Monday and I skipped my classes today. They've been playing Broken Social Scene at Bauhaus. I am so ready for soccer to end. I hate Chadwick so much, everything I do is wrong. Ugh I want to quit before season ends. I'm going to talk to my parents about it.

I want to explore Capitol Hill so badly. Every time I come here there are interesting people that inspire me. I think some people may be inspired by me. It's possible. I bleached my hair today. I'm real happy about it.

I know I have more to say but I can't think of it. I loved visiting Kan's house because it's like I know her even more, and I get to see her sisters and I think they are cool. They inspire me and make me see everything in new ways. Like when Kan wears my clothes – it makes me see the world of color and style and shape differently and I like it a lot.

I'm glad I don't have homework. That would just be too much. I don't think I could handle it. Ugh. Life is too much right now.

14 April 2011

The day before yesterday I quit the soccer team. I still don't feel it fully. After weights I had to have a meeting with Chadwick about my panic attack (of course), and he accused me of a ton of stuff, mainly having to do with me being uncoachable because of my communication problems. Which, translated to real-person speech, means that because I avoided him all the time since he is an asshole, he wasn't able to analyze my every word and thought, and therefore came to the conclusion that he can't coach me and that everything that happened was my fault entirely. God, what a dick.

Also, our assistant coach was at the meeting too, and it became this two-against-one situation where whatever I said they both denied and shut down. It started out with me having to explain why I had the panic attack, which was because literally everyone was yelling at me continuously, especially both coaches, and they both denied that that even happened. It was extremely frustrating and enraging. Like, why even have the meeting if you won't listen to me anyway? I wish they would both fucking die so I can spit on and kick the shit out of their dead bodies.

Anyway, I became kind of hysterical after that and just said everything that Chadwick has made me feel, including how he pries too much into what everyone is thinking, and how almost every person on the team has cried when they have to have meetings with him, and how he has issues with anxiety and control, and how the problem is not with us (the players on the team), it's with him. And, naturally, he denied everything and tried to twist it around so it looked like nothing was his fault (which he is *really* good at doing. It's the manipulative character of his, very convincing).

Then I said I was done. Done with soccer and dealing with him and all the shit that that entails. Then I left his office and cried in the bathroom for a while. And now it's over.

I felt bad because my parents are coming this weekend because they wanted to see me play one last time, and now they don't get to. But they are still coming. I talked to Dad on the phone and he said they would still come. Chadwick actually called Dad after our meeting and talked shit about me to him, so Dad called me right after to figure out the truth of the matter.

God, so much shit is going down, though. Kan's going to go talk to Chadwick tomorrow and if he is an asshole or doesn't cooperate then we are going to go to the athletic director. Actually, I'm going to write the athletic director an email either way, attaching my essay about Chadwick explaining everything, regardless of the outcome of Kan's meeting with him. Because Chadwick is abusive and it's not okay. He terrorizes everyone on the team and no one can really do anything about it, so we are going to try to do something about it.

Kan told me yesterday that Mila said that Chadwick's mom is bipolar! That totally explains his erratic behavior and insanity! I mean, I'm not saying people with bipolar disorder or whatever are insane, but growing up with that would definitely have a negative effect on someone. God, he's so fucked up, and he's not interested in addressing the matter.

Yesterday was the first practice I didn't attend, and it felt amazing. I'm in the process of telling all my teammates. I mean, they already know, obviously, but I want to say it in person and be able to explain my perspective.

Last night Chan and I met with Henda and talked about the fucked-upness of our school and Chadwick and everything. It was nice. Well, I have to go to my art class now.

17 April 2011

Last night there was a party at the Brick, and there weren't a million people or anything but it was still fun. A lot of the time I hung out upstairs listening to music with Trevor and

Zara. And trying to rap "Superbass" by Nicki Minaj. She is so good.

Kan got really drunk, it was awesome, ha. Trevor asked me why guys haven't fucked me. I said, "I don't know, guys just don't like me." Because they don't. Because I'm ugly. Or fucking something. He always asks hella weird questions like that when we're drunk.

Today is Sunday and I have to work in the gym. Fuck that shit. This weekend my parents were here, and we went to the game on Saturday that I would have been in. It was strange being in the stands instead of on the field. It's weird to watch my friends whom I know so fucking well play without me.

I don't know, it almost seemed natural. It was so weird that I felt like that's the way things have always been. I almost feel like all the horrors I've had to endure never happened. All the hatred of Chadwick, soccer, not knowing anyone freshman year...gone. I'm so glad it's over.

I feel like the world may start to be nice to me.* I feel like things have worked out lately, like the universe is like, "Fine, I put you through so much hell, I'll give you a little break." THANK YOU UNIVERSE, HOW KIND OF YOU! No more worrying about being in shape and being good enough and avoiding Chadwick's interrogations.

Anyway, my parents and I explored Capitol Hill and ate at this restaurant where there were SO many gay couples, it was awesome. We explored Ballard and downtown as well. They left this morning and I was sad. It was weird seeing them because I wanted to hang out with them, but at the same time I also wanted to be with my soccer friends and be drunk. It was like a tension of desire in my mind.

I cut myself last night in my dorm room and put the blood in my sketchbook. I tried to cut myself at the Brick but I couldn't find anything sharp enough.

I am so excited to study abroad. I have to. I will if it's the last thing I do. I have to get out of North America.

[*Ana: Lol, that'll last like five minutes. Saturn rules everything about you baby, get used to suffering. Or rather, try to make peace with the inevitable. –J.]

20 April 2011

It's 8:43 a.m. and I just had my Social Psych exam. It went well. I was one of the first to finish. I thought it was hella easy.

I have been needing to write very badly lately, but every time I get out my journal I can't remember what I wanted to say.

Yesterday I studied at Starbucks with Kan and Zara. Kan is thinking about transferring because she can't play for Chadwick and she can't stand that he did what he did to me. I can't believe I have a best friend. I never thought I had any friends.

Now that I don't have soccer I feel like such a real person. I have so much time on my hands to do whatever, it's the best. The other day it was real sunny and nice out so I went on a run and then rode my bike around Gasworks and painted in my sketchbook. It was so beautiful, it's what people are supposed to do. They are supposed to say, "I wonder what I'll do today?" And then do whatever they feel like. It's revolutionary.

I was and still am always thinking about jobs and what I feel would be a fulfilling job. And I seriously can't think of anything, except to learn more, always to learn more about the world and the mind and other people. I think exploring and having adventures should help the learning process. Being street smart is good, too.

Everything has been fast paced lately. I feel like I haven't just been still. Maybe I'm making all of this up. I feel good about not doing soccer anymore. Before I quit I was struggling so hard with not being with my teammates anymore, but I think I am over it. I think another thing that was hard for me was admitting that I couldn't handle something, and I think that's because I'm so goddamn proud. Well, I was. I don't know if I still am.

I think it felt so good being broken. Being unable to handle something and being able to admit it. I think that's what I always wanted: failure, so I could know that somehow I'm important, because it implies so much emotion and human fragility. I just felt such a release after being in Chadwick's office crying and hysterical. It's all over now, things can only get better from here. No one can be worse than Chadwick, so I don't have to worry about people ever again. I think I'm just excited about the future, and I feel much freer.

Ana + Kan = Kana. The story of our lives: Wanting to know the truth when others won't acknowledge it. Others won't acknowledge the tension created by perceptual imbalance – conflict between thoughts, emotions, behavior. Anxiety and depression are forms of perceptual imbalance. You have to talk to others about it and form healthy relationships by working through shit you can't work through by yourself. Chadwick is so fucked up that he deliberately ignores the truth; he wraps it in anger and denial and the desire for control.

Today is coffee, time, calories, shoulds, sunny, coldish, downtown, breeze, green tipped trees, good outfit, tired, taking pictures, reading about the adolescent mind for my Psych class, people I wish existed, people I wish didn't exist, 4/20, wasting time, poems I wish I could create, solitary, everyone is solitary, a working iPod, Zara's soft voice proclaiming she doesn't know what she's doing, doesn't want to do anything, me having nothing to do so becoming anxious because I "should" work out. Fuck that word, "should."

Seattle's not the same when it's sunny. It's strange and it makes me feel like I'm in the wrong place. I need to be different, independent, creative, mysterious, sultry, Courtney Love, writing, learning, *revolution*, excited about the future. I need love, I need someone to kiss, someone to exploit, someone to take risks with.

Release, another world, another time, another me. Your memory a small seed of thought, planted and watered and protected. Bodies moving against and together in a world of colored hair and mourning the deaths of gods once believed in. There is no god, only a yearning for security, only a cowardly willingness to be dependent, to shield what you don't want to see, a thin veil of insignificant meaningfulness. I'm a hypocrite and scared into respectfulness.

This makes me like myself. Like yourself, goddamnit! Notebooks, papers, diary entries, lists, shampoos, lotions, baby powder, accessories, jewelry, clothes, messy, talking. I'm famous, I'm fucking famous, night, ugly drawings, slanted writing, looking in the wrong places.

Do it, do it, listen to your own breathing, feel the pulsing and pounding and leg twitches and cars. Pretend the rushing of the cars and the atmosphere is the ocean, breathing you in, crushing your mind's outcry. Don't cry, sob. Hate yourself, cut yourself, destruction, devastation, you're stupid and worthless, nothing to lose, give it all, take it, keep it hidden in a heart shaped box.

Blood on your wrists, sexual and full-lipped, vibrant, luscious, struggling, bubbling to the surface in small skin fissures. Scabs in lines and cracks. Kiss it, caress it, it's you and you love yourself, you hate yourself so much that you love yourself. What is wrong with me?

21 April 2011

Yesterday we got high at the Brick for 4/20. I'm still there, it's nine in the morning. It's sunny outside. I hope it stays for the majority of the day. We started watching *Horton Hears A Who*, and it was so weird to watch high. It was funny.

I don't know how I feel about myself. Because I don't like myself when I'm around Cameron, because I feel like she's mean to me. Not really, maybe I just take it that way when I'm high. I don't know. And she is super nice with Kan and I get so jealous and then feel stupid for feeling jealous. And worthless.

I need ART. I need to save all the thoughts and feelings and memories and words. Am I trapped by this desire? I want immortality.*

[*Ana: You want to be loved by the undying. You want to be admired by Time itself, the night owl cloaked in starry darkness, sipping on infinity. –J.]

24 April 2011

Today is Easter Sunday. I've had a relaxing morning. I read poetry while drinking left over coffee from last night. I am excited for today because all I have to do is read a book for Psych.

Yesterday I went to watch our game with the junior soccer

guys. Zara and I walked to their house before and hung out in the front yard because it was sunny and warm.

Oh, I dyed parts of my hair black, like the tips and part of my bangs. It's, like, more than the tips, though. Like almost half of it, as if I dipped it halfway into a bucket of night. I think I like it because everyone keeps telling me how much they love it, haha. I don't know. I was doubtful at first, but not really anymore. It's been a couple days since I did it, and I still haven't washed it. I'm trying to see how long I can go before it gets gross.

26 April 2011

There are days when I wake up and I just can't deal with this shit. This Christian shit. All these ignorant people, I can't stand them. Every person I see holding a Bible makes me feel violent. I want to rip it apart and scream at them, "There is no fucking God, quit trying to comfort yourselves!!" I have to get out of here. I don't know what I'm doing and I never get what I want. And I want something else if I do get it.

TAKE RISKS.

Now I'm tired. I don't know what my life is for or what to do or if something is good quality or not. I don't know how I feel. I'm at a coffee shop by Pike Place. I've caught two people staring openly at me. A teen boy and an old woman. They all look at me like I'm some exotic creature. I dunno if I like it or not.

Today's sunny and beautiful and I'm a terrible person for not enjoying it. I'm in a bad mood. The future seems like a shit-hole. I keep looking too far ahead. I see this summer, perhaps jobless and in Boise – the worst thing. I can't stay in Seattle if

I don't get a job. And I don't want to talk to anyone, which is what applying for jobs entails.

I hate that I can't talk. I mean, I can, but what I hate is that it makes me uncomfortable. It sucks because that's just who I am. I don't think I can fix it. I'm just naturally quiet, naturally reserved until I really get to know people. I'm just *introverted*. You can't change that with drugs. Sorry Zoloft, you make me feel a little less anxious when dealing with people, but you don't do shit for my motivation. Fuck it all. I'll be jobless because I'm socially incompetent.

I'll never have any goddamn British friends. And yeah, I'm going to study abroad in London! Fuck yeah. What after, though? Back to Boise again? Fuck that. Why does that have to be my home base? I'm too tired to figure out what I want to do. It's too hard, there are too many options. Fuck this life.

Love,

Stupid Girl

P.S. I'm a terrible artist. And yes, I know I have blatant cognitive distortions.

28 April 2011

I've been reading travel tips for studying abroad and I'm so excited. HOLY FUCK, I'm going to London. Please universe, let it work out. Be nice to me for once.

The last soccer game is tonight. Trevor's going to drive Zara and I there.

02 May 2011

Lately I haven't known what I'm feeling at all.

I wrote Kan a poem the other day about how I miss her even when I am with her, and she wrote one back that made me cry. I just felt so sad that I'm leaving her. I cried on the balcony of my dorm.

I don't know anything anymore. I've been so fucking tired lately. I took a three hour and forty minute long nap yesterday, and I still could've gone to bed at, like, midnight or so, when I usually do.

Last night Kan and I watched *The Girl Who Kicked the Hornet's Nest*. It made me feel better. I should watch more movies because it's an escape. I imagine being there and having an adventure.

I wish I could remember the messages from books, movies, and music that have made me feel like things are going to be okay. Because I always forget them and I hate it because I need them in order to like myself, or be happy, or, I dunno, some shit.

05 May 2011

Today = art class. It wasn't horrible because we watched videos and it wasn't too boring.

Yesterday I was super anxious all day because I felt fat and I didn't work out at all, and I didn't know what to do and I had stuff I could do but didn't do, and I just hated myself. God, it sucked. But last night we watched TV and I edited my book and it was okay.

I also went to Forever 21 with Lillian yesterday and bought a Hello Kitty tank top, a polka dot bra, and long feather earrings. I felt really guilty and anxious for spending money. I felt fat and ugly because I hated my outfit and I didn't fit into any of the other things I tried on.

Also, I feel guilty because there are some clothes I have that I never wear, for no apparent reason since I really like them. Like the purple dress from Urban Outfitters that I wore to Maddie's wedding. I never wear that! So I wore it today to feel less guilty. And it was expensive, so I feel bad that I don't wear it, like, every day. I like it a lot so I don't know what's wrong with me. I dunno why, but that has just been bugging the shit out of me. I can't stop thinking about it. I think I'm insane.

I have been freaking out about jobs and being really worried and anxious about it, and I can't figure out why. I don't know if I really want to stay here for summer or not, because I wanted to get a job and stay here so I won't have to go back to Boise and hate myself.

Maybe it's the city that makes me anxious. And having to compete with people for jobs that I don't want as much as they do and am not qualified for. It just feels pointless and I want to hide in my shell in the dark and not talk to anyone. It's stupid.

Maybe I am just sick of the city and need to go live in nature for a while. I think the competition thing is a huge part of it for some reason. Ugh, I'm so annoyed, I really am annoyed at life. I don't have a good reason for wanting a job either – besides money, which I don't even need as much as I think I do because I try to never spend it. I just feel like I'm inadequate and I'll always be inadequate and that I'll be homeless. I want to know that I can take care of myself. I don't know why it's such a big deal. FUCK.

Tonight I'm going to the EMP to see the Nirvana exhibit with Drake, Trevor, and Mila. I love Kurt.

08 May 2011

I have not been feeling good. Yesterday I stayed in bed until 1:20 p.m. because I was feeling so anxious and pointless. The night before I cut my wrists twice while I was drunk. I don't know what's wrong with me. I have been so tired and I don't want to do anything.

Today I work in the gym for four hours, which should be okay because I don't have to deal with that many people. I feel like I'm in high school. I feel like I'm falling apart. My body hurts, I'm super tight and stretching doesn't help. I went on a run yesterday and I think that made me feel better. Not sure.

I've started reading *Extremely Loud and Incredibly Close*, and I think I like it a lot.

I've been freaking out about money. I think I need some goddamn sedatives. I can't figure out if I want to be happy. I don't like my boring, stupid life. There is too much shit in my head and I hate all of these people because they are normal and conventional and complacent and perfectly happy to OBEY.

I don't like being human. I think I'm breaking down. Slowly. It's because for the first time in my life I'm allowed to be a person, I don't have to be the best and be perfect and success-ful. Soccer here (Chadwick) made me feel like that, always. I hate it I hate it I hate it I hate everything.

Worker bees, should statements, filling up the page, wanting to connect with people but not at the same time because then my aloneness is not mine or special anymore, blank space, point-lessness, perfectionism, alone as good, alone as bad, summer, summer, dread, Idaho, fuck fuck fuck, I don't want to be there but I don't want to be here, I think I know myself and then I realize I don't and I don't know what I'm doing anymore.

Did I ever know what I was doing?

I talked to Mom on the phone and told her that I'm coming home for summer and that I want to talk to my doctor about getting a higher dosage of Zoloft. I feel like she makes me feel reassured because she acts like it's not that big of a deal, but then at the same time I feel like she should be more concerned, and that makes me anxious. I think she thinks that it's normal to be really anxious about stuff, and I don't think it is. I don't know anything. But I do know that I want to come home for summer and I want to know that things are okay and that I'm safe. I don't want to be there forever, just for a little while. Fucking shit.

10 May 2011

I like my outfit today. I love when I like my outfits because it gives me the best vibes ever and I feel like a real person.

I took my Adolescent Psych test on Monday and I have my Social Psych one tomorrow. I don't have much homework other than studying for that, so I should be feeling free. But I don't because I feel like I should run absolutely every day and that makes me feel trapped. I feel like I should be running because I hate my stomach so much.

I don't know what I'm doing…ever…I'm searching for a feeling. I'm searching for a feeling!

12 May 2011

I was just talking to one of the freshman girls on my team about studying abroad, and I am jealous because she went to Europe during the summer because she has great connections with lots of people. I wish I had great connections. I guess if I could just ask people to hang out then maybe I'd have great connections. Fuck.

I don't know what my life is for. I really hope I make friends in London. I'm going to fucking London! Shit, I want it to work, please let it work.

16 May 2011

Monday. Yesterday I had a good day, and it was the first time I've had a good day in a long while. It's because I drank a whole pot of coffee in the morning and was bzzzing on caffeine. Also, I took a huge shit because of that, wahoo!

Then I worked in the gym and while I was there I wrote almost all of this six to eight page paper that's due in, like, two weeks. It was making me anxious so I feel better now. Then Kan and I went on a run around Gasworks. And I was in a good mood the whole time! Weird.

I couldn't fall asleep last night so I listened to Rage Against the Machine, and Zack de la Rocha's voice is the best. I adore him.

Maybe today I should go somewhere. They never have any bus passes at the student union building anymore, it pisses me off. My throat hurts.

20 May 2011

Sick. Sick as in unhealthy. Sick of classes, sick of homework, sick of people, especially girls, sick of thinking, sick of anxiety, sick of this school, sick of myself, sick of trying, sick of everything. Ugh.

Today I skipped Social Psych. Two weeks until I leave this place forever. So excited. All I want to do is sleep and never exist. I don't know what else.

21 May 2011

A veil of rain. Sheets of thin tracing paper covering the bridges and the buildings, brightening the greens and shading the city lights. I miss you when I'm with you and I hate you and I hate my anxiety. I want your clean coolness to myself, alone and free and secret.

The sun exposes everything: my guilt for not being happy, my attempts at extroversion failed, my stupid hatred, my boredom, my refusal to conform, my longing search for a similar soul. Failure, failure, stupid fucking shithole Boise. Too anxious to do what I want, too anxious to disobey, to rebel, to take risks, to make decisions, to do anything. Too anxious to live.

I want to sleep forever in an old graveyard under the grass. No computer screens. No talking, no feeling, no wanting, no disappointment, no feeling like you deserve what you get. No feeling bad for no fucking reason. No nothing. No trying to be nice and look like I enjoy the situations I'm in.

The depths of the ocean, the magnitude of mystery, the swallowing silent wisdom, the shimmering fat beauty of infinite knowledge, never ending, growing, pulsing, complex, frightening, freezing insanity, out of proportion, stretching the limits of this tiny, frail computer, worry, worrying, right and wrong, should, confusion, what I want, what I need, solitude, loneliness, understanding, lover, vicious, underground society, a part of something, no, never a part of anything, apathy, how some movements are strange when your mind is twisted in poison, we love our poison, freaking out, too many things.

TRAPPED. I need out, let me out, get me out of here, where am I? Am I making this up? Am I the product of chemical imbalance? Will you think I'm crazy if I tell you what I really feel? Eating, sleeping, eating, sleeping, same cycle, break it, crush it, obliteration, hurt yourself if you think you want to. Walking, moving, feeling, rushing, there's too much, I love how we keep all this energy wasted inside. I think my energy wastes itself, afraid to go anywhere because I'll run out of fuel.

Pretending I'm happy, I'm faking it for others' sake, don't want to hurt their fragile fucking feelings, you know? Don't want Mom to think I'm not her perfect angel, that I'm actually fucked up for no reason. Probably making it all up, I want to be bad but I'm too anxious, too nervous.

Now I'm drained, now I can't feel anything. Coffee's not even making me like myself like it usually does. Except I strangely like myself, in a fucked up way, like when you want to squeeze something to death because you love it too much.

I'm scared because I don't think I'm okay. Drunk = okay. Normal = bad.

22 May 2011

Last night I got drunk in my room alone and pierced my own nose. It looks hella good. Kan came over after a while and was my moral support. I'm really glad I did that because now I can say I pierced my own nose. Who does that?

Yesterday sucked. Zara and I went to the Green House for a bit and hung out, and then I went to this graveyard and explored and held the darkness in my mind with the song of the birds and the green leaves covering the sky. Kan and I stole this girl's ice cream from the community fridge on my floor and ate all of it. It wasn't even open. I hate her so I'm glad we did it.

Mom called me this morning and told me that Grandpa died. So that's sad. Dad's dad. Weird. I think I just don't understand the concept of death because it never makes me particularly sad. Then I think I'm a bad person for feeling nothing.

Undated, May 2011

it's all that emotion, communication, questions, personality disorders, time, space, quantum mechanics, my tattoos, your voice, words, typewriters, inventions, toilets, rings, theft, headaches, traveling, egolessness, your opinions, my confusion, everyone's dreadfulness, the law of gravity, existence, swimming, our stupid fucking chemical imbalances, POISON make me feel okay, perspective, perspective, a thought filling up the room, stealing my air, I can't breathe I can't move, panic, silence, immovable, frozen,

let go, insanity, connections between emotion and thought, movies, balloons, change, design, philosophy, exercise, books, don't judge a fuckin' book by its cover, assholes stealing the resources, time, space, physics, mysteries, uncertainty, shyness, professors, you, everyone you know, countries, tears, education, us, dresses, food, scissors, lists, ugly poetry, uselessness, meaninglessness, monsters, journals, personality disorders, black and white, boredom, teeth, cutting, learning, manipulating, alone in our own heads, my soul is reaching out to yours, infinity, balance, packing, collections, styles, cigarettes, nature, hands, sleep, clouds, the global economy, my secret universe, ignorance, hopelessness, the cognitive machine, people, hurt, post scripts, stamps, resumes, talking, following society blindly, you, me, we as one, we are one, questions, drugs, needles, summer, parents, shoes, seconds ticking away, signaling the end of my fruition, my desire, my ideas, my chances, my insecurities, my love, my shame, my stupid lack of whatever I want,

disease, opportunity, fear, choice, running away from your problems, how do you know if you're a bad person?, if you have a question I may have an answer, stereotypes, working, killing gluttony, busy, subtle, work, names, categories, destruction, holidays, hiding, typography, charts, fireworks, not letting people know what you're thinking, trains, time, space, us, we, you, me, crying, hugging, separating, bleeding, blood, dirt, tragedy, my universe, fashion, filth, magazines, pencils, stars, lakes, stars reflecting in lakes,

a universe contained in small watery tears, boxes, heart-shaped boxes, lust, longing, birds, blasphemy, lying, three dimensions, video games, time, space, anxiety, nostalgia for the things you never had, clay, salt, nail polish, eccentricities, criticality, words that don't exist, you don't exist, I won't exist for you but I would die for you, seeds sown with expectation, uncomfortable situations that aren't uncomfortable but for the faulty perceptions of your fragile psyche, musical instruments, being let down, rearranging the furniture,

boring classes, waking up early, too early, lying in the clouds, pulling the sun up like a marionette with white fishing line and a smile as bright as the newborn rays, strengthening your calves by wearing high heels, dynamite, dirt, smooth skin, freckles, babies, ovens, record players, pain, the menstrual cycle, lost, finite, floating, jumping, triangles, length, you, me, despair, obliteration, Europe as a safe place, a place of sanity, a hospital room with soothing walls, lips,

26 May 2011

In Social Psych we learned about attachment styles, and I discovered (I think) that my adult attachment style is insecure avoidant, which means I fear getting close to others, don't trust others, and am cynical about the world and relationships. This totally explains why I don't think I have friends, why I don't perceive my relationships as meaningful even when they are, and why I can't talk to people or ask for help even when I really need it.

I'm going to talk to Mom about what I was like as an infant, because I want to know if my infant attachment style was also insecure avoidant or if I was securely attached. Because if I was securely attached I don't know why I would have an avoidant adult style now.

I can't wait to leave forever. I also can't wait to pack for London and figure out what I'm taking. It's going to be a great adventure. I don't want to come back. I want to work behind the scenes in a movie, or a project, or an art installation, or something special and exclusive. I want to know that I'm special.

I want to be good at something. I want to be admired. I want people to be influenced by what I say, at their own risk. I want nice arms and no love handles and to love all my clothes as much as they love me, and see them in a new light each day, as if I had just seen them for the first time in the store and fallen for them, and had to have them. I want to feel the way I feel about the people in the movies and books about myself when I wear my outfits.

28 May 2011

9:54 p.m., drinking very strong coffee at Kan's parent's house. She and her older sister are watching a movie on my laptop in their younger sister's room, and I am at the counter in the kitchen rubbing the noise of the refrigerator all over my body, a mechanical lotion, a soft, rolling, mumbling presence.

Today Kan and I got piercings together. I got two rings on my ear cartilage and she got her septum, it looks hella tight. We are getting tattoos tomorrow. We have an appointment at 3:30 p.m. *Kana*. I want to get seahorses on my right arm because I think they are mystical and mysterious and Kurt Cobain liked them and they are saying fuck you to norms and sexism because the male gives birth.

29 May 2011

In Portland! Drinking coffee, hot, drip. Gray evening sky. Typing keys, overheard conversations, almost dizzy buzzing. Second cup of coffee, refills only 50 cents. We got tattoos on our ankles – *Kana*. So tight, so fucking tight.

Today we went on a hike in the morning with Kan's family. In the woods, soggy, cool, hidden, wind created by fast feet. It was lovely. I was running, it felt so good. After that we came to Portland and got our tattoos. They look real great. And we look fabulous today. We are both wearing high heels with socks. I'm glad I bought these shoes because it's easy to walk around in them and they don't hurt my feet.

I think all I have to do for school is study. I'm totes done with my Social Psych paper, but it's one page too long, oops. God, I am so goddamn excited to go home and to do summer school and to work out and to like myself? I like myself right now because I'm high on caffeine and I'm wearing a great outfit and I have a kickass badass best friend like I've always wanted. Seriously I always wrote about that and now I have it.

Words: sizzle, corporeal, frenetic, origin, despot,

31 May 2011

Downtown Seattle. Sitting in the sun where they play those life size chess matches. Long jean skirt, new high heels, flannel. I'm skipping dinner at the cafeteria because I'm anxious and I want to be able to just do nothing. I'm not really hungry because I ate snacks, and I hate my body. I have a huge underground zit on my forehead.

The seagulls remind me of the ocean and the Oregon coast, where we used to vacation when I was little, and where I haven't been in forever. I live in Seattle and I never go to the beach, or see the ocean. I think it might be just a bay or something, not the vast infinite darkness I fear and long for.

I get anxious about running. I suppose that is something I should tell the psychiatrist when I get one. I don't feel like the people in the books and that's all I want to feel like. Last night I dreamt that Henda brought Kan and I to a street fight and we took turns fighting random people we didn't know. I was running around Pike Place and people were looking at me admirably because I won all the fights, and Mark, this guy I have a crush on that works in the cafeteria, was there. It was just weird.

I thought about why I am anxious about working out and my body. I'm anxious about working out because it makes me feel trapped because I have to do it regularly in order for it to be effective, and I want to be free and do whatever I want without a schedule. That's why the cafeteria makes me anxious, because they only serve food at certain hours, and it's also why I'm skipping it right now. But, at the same time, I don't like my body – particularly my stomach, and I feel guilty every time I'm eating because I'm not working out regularly. It doesn't help that I pick the worst food choices ever and love eating.

Well, enough about that. Do I have fucking OCD or what?

I want to say that I like Portland better than Seattle. I think all the things that have happened to me, or didn't happen to me, were for a reason. Like not being able to find a job here, hating Chadwick and soccer and my school, not even finding a fucking boy to hang out with. I mean, I found Syler, kind of, but he had to leave Washington to go to university in Idaho. That's why we stopped hanging out. But I think it's because Seattle wasn't meant to be. It was my first love, but it didn't work out, and maybe that's good. Maybe this is not where I belong.

I also want to say that I think my birth control is making me gain weight. I hate that. Fucking stupid, why do I have to hate my body so much?

Well, I just got asked if I am homeless by this homeless guy that looked like an extremely Asian version of Dave Grohl. Ha, that's awesome because I'm totally into the home-less/grunge look.

I guess I'll go back to school and kill everyone. Fucking fuck. I wonder if I'll hate everyone no matter where I go? God, so much negativity. I need to acquire me some more fucking Zoloft. Or some shit.

06 June 2011

Home. Finally. I got home Saturday, the drive was okay. I slept a lot, didn't even listen to music.

Currently I am at the Boise library downtown. I'm taking summer school and I had my first class – Statistics. It was all right. In an hour I have Personality Psych.

It's weird because I hate Idaho but downtown Boise is okay. I like that it's less crowded than Seattle because I can find a parking spot easily and for free. I got a summer membership to the YMCA so I am going to swim all the time and have nice arms.

Today I have an appointment with my gynecologist and I am going to ask him for a referral to a psychiatrist. I seriously think I have a personality disorder. I don't know. Kan did, why wouldn't I? Oh my god, did I ever tell you that she was diagnosed with borderline personality disorder? I don't think I did! Isn't that crazy? It's totally fine though, she's not insane or anything. It's just her patterns of thinking, kind of, and issues around impulsivity.

She sees a lot of things in black and white. Like, it's hard for her to realize that things can have both good and bad parts to them, or that things don't have only one side to them. I dunno, she knows things rationally but emotionally she doesn't feel it. It's hard to explain.

08 June 2011

At the public library again. Yesterday I sent my personal

essay to Chadwick and the athletic director. I was so fucking anxious yesterday because I was waiting to see what Chadwick would say, and also because the athletic director replied and said that the main athletic coordinator or something was going to contact me, and I was afraid she'd call me and I'd have to talk on the phone. Chadwick still hasn't replied and now I don't even care if he does. I'm not anxious about that anymore.

I had an appointment with my gynecologist and he referred me to a psychiatrist, so I still have to call and make an appointment, which I'm afraid to do. Oh, he also upped my Zoloft dosage, thank god.

I decided to write out some symptoms to tell the psychiatrist:

Concerning people:

I can't talk to people, I can't let people in, I can't open up to people, I don't trust people even when I try to. I get anxious when I have to speak – like presentations or interviews or meeting new people or talking to people at all. I feel socially awkward and I end up hating myself when I say something and feel awkward. I don't want to talk to people because they're not real, they don't get it, they're not genuine.

I can't talk on the phone, it makes me too nervous – even making appointments is hard. I never contact friends first, I never call people, I never ask people to hang out. Avoidant personality – cynical about relationships, I don't trust people because no matter what they'll always betray you. And it's human nature to care about yourself first, so how can I trust people if they will always put themselves first? I can't ask for help even when I need it. I don't feel like a real person because I can't talk to people.

Concerning the future:

I worry A LOT about jobs and living arrangements and getting enough to eat and how I'm going to get where I need to go and where I'm going to sleep and whether I'll be able to wash my face and brush my teeth. It's just dumb. I don't need to worry about that right now, but I obsessively worry and am anxious about this stuff. I think way too far ahead. I feel like I have to get a job to support myself and I don't even want one because nothing sounds fulfilling or worth my time.

Concerning myself:

I get extremely anxious when I don't work out every day because I feel like I'm going to get fat. I hate my stomach more than anything. I hate my face and my stupid huge nose.

I doubt myself for no reason – I'm smart, I'm liked. I don't like myself a lot, but then sometimes I do like myself and I am proud of myself.

I started cutting at school. It made me feel like a real person because it meant taking risks and I never took risks when I was younger because I was too anxious. I haven't done it in a while. I don't think it's a big deal because I'm not suicidal. I did it when I was indecisive because it was a decision that I invested in and went through with.

I have no confidence or faith – why try when there's always going to be someone better than you? I don't think I am good enough anyway. I don't think I'm good enough to get a job because I can't seem to find one. I don't think I'll ever be good enough for things, or that I'll ever be able to talk to people and not feel stupid.

I don't think I'll ever be happy because everything's pointless and I don't know what I want, and if I get what I want I don't want it anymore, and everything makes me feel trapped. My anxiety, Boise, people, schedules, jobs, money – it's all a prison.* I feel trapped, like I can't just go explore the places where I am. I do explore, but I feel anxious and like everyone is looking at me. I force myself to explore because I want to want to explore. But I always feel trapped.*

[*Ana: Reflections of your 12th house everything. Also, your moon is conjunct Uranus. You crave novelty, adventure, infinitely strange and quixotic stimuli, freedom. But the 12th house and Saturn…How will you resolve these paradoxes? –J.]

I can't ask for help, no matter what, I can't do it. I try to always be self-reliant and I feel like a failure if I have to ask for help. It's hard for me to tell people something's wrong. I feel like I should just get over it, or push through it and be better than my mind.

I can't spend money, it makes me too anxious. And then I can't enjoy whatever it is I spent money on because I worry too much about the fact that I have less money after buying something.

All I want to do is sleep or not exist.

I just want to be by myself for forever because that would be safe. But I don't like it at the same time, and I want to have friends but I just can't talk to people because I don't trust them and I don't think they're real.

Concerning the Now:

I don't know what's going on anymore. I don't know what I'm doing with my life, I don't know who I am. I don't care about anything. I've lost motivation. I just want to give up and lay on the ground and die. And make Mom do everything for me.

I'm really tired all the time. I take more than an hour nap and then still go to bed at around midnight when I would normally. I've been sleeping through my alarm and I don't realize when I turn it off.

Occasional headaches. There are too many things. There is so much shit in my head that I can't figure out. Like psychological stuff, like why people do things and how I feel about different things and whether people are inherently good or not. I can't explain how I'm feeling and I'm confused about my feelings.

I get anxious when I have a schedule, but if I don't have anything I get SO bored and then anxious because I feel like I should be doing something. I always feel this way. I can't just sit around and do nothing or relax because I think about all the things I should be doing. I feel like I should be productive or work out or enjoy something, and when I don't I feel guilty.

Nothing sounds fun anymore. I don't want to do anything, and then I get really anxious because I need to be doing something at all times, or being productive somehow, or multitasking, but it all sounds so shitty, and then I can't move and I just sit there immobilized being anxious because I don't want to do anything, but I want to want to do something. It's just circles and circles of paralyzing anxiety.

I don't like Boise because I feel like everyone is a redneck and isn't doing anything worthwhile with his life, and it makes me feel unsafe. I never feel safe and I think I would feel safe if I were with people that are successful or intelligent or know what they're doing or where they're going, or are better than me at things I want to be better at because then I could learn from them. But there is no one.

Sometimes things seem hopeless – like it's not worth trying

for because it'll never work out. I get frustrated easily and just feel like giving up. I hate that I have to go through with things that seem pointless or hopeless even when I know they're not. Like filling out forms for studying abroad, picking class schedules, and transferring my credits when they don't transfer perfectly.

Caffeine makes it better, makes me like myself, makes me excited for the future. Alcohol has the same effects but I don't overuse. I'm too anxious to overuse. I wish I could overuse. I wish my anxiety wouldn't make me so responsible. I wish I could make mistakes or do things wrong or make my parents mad or disappointed. But I can't do it. I am afraid to do what I really want to do.

I'm afraid of insanity. I'm afraid that there is an ultimate right or wrong and that I'm doing everything wrong and that I'm crazy. I'm afraid to feel better because somehow feeling shitty is poetic or significant or better than how other people feel. I'm trapped by these fears and it's the worst. I feel like I'm making it all up and it's not even happening and that I'm overreacting and everyone feels like this, except everyone else just deals with it.

12 June 2011

It's Sunday and I'm eating watermelon and studying Statistics. My parents are doing yard work. We are going to see *Hanna* at the dollar theatre.

This morning we talked to Sawyer and Lacy on Skype, but we couldn't see their faces because our home computer doesn't have a webcam thing. They are in Thailand and were about to go to bed. I think now it's almost three in the morning their time.

Chadwick never emailed me back, and the main athletic coordinator didn't either. GOOD, I am so over it. I just wanted to email him so I can let it go. Not my problem anymore.

13 June 2011

I'm in a coffee shop downtown. There are only three other people here. Quiet. I just got out of Personality Psych. It's interesting but it's so long that I get bored. I had a Stats test and I think it went well…not sure. I probably made stupid mistakes.

It's sunny and breezy outside, warmish. I wonder if I have a fear of open spaces. No, no I don't. I just can't figure out why Boise makes me so uncomfortable!

I didn't go to the Y right after class like I usually do because I wanted to stay downtown since I haven't been hanging out down here after my classes. I haven't because I feel like I should work out right away and get home. But then I realized I don't want to go home because there's nothing to do except random chores, or getting my lists all crossed off. And I don't want to do that. I want to be a real person and just hang out downtown or do whatever I want. Because I really don't have to do anything. I tell myself that I should do things, but I don't really have to do them.

There are two kinds of "shoulds." The first is shoulds that I don't have to do if I don't want to, but I still feel like I need to do, and the second is shoulds that I want to want to do because normal people would get enjoyment out of it. For example: I told myself that I should stay downtown today and go to a coffee shop, which is what I wanted to want to do, the second should.

I feel like I just don't even want to do anything anymore.

Nothing sounds like an awesome idea. It's weird and I don't like it. And going to the Y right after class is the first should, the one that I don't have to do if I don't want to, but it would be healthy or is necessary. And that makes me anxious.

I feel like I'm in the middle of fucking nowhere. And these people know nothing. It's stupid, it may be irrational, I don't know if I need it or not. I just feel like I need to be anywhere else than here. Anywhere else would be better. FUCK MY LIFE. I want to be real so badly, I want it more than anything. Who am I? What the fuck am I doing here?

18 June 2011

I'm at a bookstore. I studied Stats and did a few Personality Psych journals. I went shopping with Mom today. I drank two cups of coffee this morning. I feel like I can't get anything done at home, it's so annoying. That's why I'm here.

Kan and I created a Kana blog. I think it's so cool. It's only for us, so we can write to each other and keep everything saved. We only have two posts right now. It fucking sucks we can't be together at all moments…haha.

I was supposed to see a psychiatrist on Thursday but my insurance doesn't pay for that particular place, so I cancelled and I am going to ask my gyno to refer me to a different place. I am nervous about that.

I am supposed to start my period in a couple days, which I think makes me super negative and I ALWAYS hate myself during it. I realized this last night because I fell asleep wanting to cry over how fucking ugly I think I am, and how much I hate my stupid, boring, meaningless life. God, it sucked so bad. I could just feel the negative emotions washing over me, drowning me, cluttering up my mind with useless and irrational thoughts. There's nothing I can do about it, which may be the worst part. Oh, well. Oh fucking well. It's stupid.

27 June 2011

Mom and I went to Lewiston after my classes last Thursday and I had a really good time. I think I needed it for my mental health. I love being around Camila because she always makes me laugh and makes me feel better, and I always have good adventures with her.

I met her new boyfriend, Wade. He is nice. We had a party at his house and I played beer pong with their friend Reid and we were beating everyone. It was crazy because I'm the worst at beer pong! He called me Hello Kitty because I was wearing a Hello Kitty shirt, but he thought my real name was Jem because that's what Camila told him it was, when really that's her mom's cat's name. Haha. He kept calling me Hello Kitty and then being like, "Don't worry, I know your real name is Jem!" I just laughed really hard and never told him my real name.

The next night we celebrated half-Christmas, but there weren't as many people. I visited Weston's new apartment, which is within walking distance of Wade's house, and it was so fucking awesome! He only has to pay, like, 200 dollars a month, and he has his own tiny area and a kitchen. We took shots with a couple of their friends that live next door. They are all so nice.

I kissed Weston, which I always do when I'm drunk around him. He told me I was beautiful, and I told him all I wanted was to be genuine, and he told me that's exactly what I am, and that made me feel like things were going to be okay. He tried to make me dance with him, like the formal type of dancing, and it was horrible because I can't dance.

Syler texted me because he's taking summer school at the university in Moscow and so he is in Idaho for the summer, and Camila had told him I was in Lewiston, but we didn't get to hang out. I wish we could have. I want to go back for a couple weeks or something so I can hang out with him. I want to fuck him. And just get it over with before I go to London. Because I really want his body and I don't like being a virgin, for some unknown reason. It annoys me.

Anyway, I also met Camila's dog and she's the most cooperative dog ever. She rode in Camila's purse while we rode her scooter, it was so funny. We just stuffed her in there and she didn't seem bothered at all.

Last night when Mom and I got home we made plans – to camp and fish, and to have a yard sale, and to do all these things, and it made me excited for the future. And it was the weirdest feeling because I never feel excited. At least lately.

03 July 2011

The day before yesterday my uncle died. Dad's older brother. DIED. WHAT THE FUCK. I guess he crashed his dirt bike or something and broke his neck. It's awful. Dad was crying and I was crying and trying to console him.

The next day Dad drove to Utah, where his brother's family lives, so our camping trip that we were going to go on was cancelled. I feel so bad. The whole situation is just fucked up. I keep thinking if it had been Sawyer, I would be devastated. I can't even imagine having a sibling die. I don't even want to imagine.

It's weird though, because I didn't know my uncle very well, and that whole side of my family is pretty distant and we rarely see them. I think I was more upset at the fact that Dad was so upset and it just felt really fucked up. I honestly don't think I've ever seen Dad cry before.

04 July 2011

Things I want: to buy my own wine in London since the drinking age is 18 and not 21, to only have a few things, my favorite things. To live somewhere with good vibes. No furniture, mattress on the floor. To always have that tipsy feeling, when you start to feel the alcohol but can act perfectly normal. To read everything, to be inspired, to inspire, to be real. To be someone else, everyone else.

I am only repeating myself by writing these lines. I always say the same thing, I always bear the same message when I write in my journals.

05 July 2011

Today is fucking hot! It sucks. I'm at a coffee shop downtown. Just got out of class, boring as usual. I like riding my bike. I have nothing good to say, just blah. Blah, which is my life.

Everyone in Boise has the UGLIEST tattoos. Like, I keep seeing a ton of people just downtown and their tattoos are so fucking ugly. It drives me crazy.

I think everyone is boring. The workers here are bad at making coffee. I'm going to read *Harry Potter* now because I hate my life and wish to escape.

07 July 2011

Right now I am drinking tea in my room. Mom and Dad are asleep. This is exactly what I should be doing and I feel like a real person! Weird!

Today was my last day of summer school. I had two tests.

Tomorrow we are having our yard sale. I am so excited. I got my purple trunk from the storage unit and went through everything in it and got rid of stuff, and I put other stuff I had been saving in it, and it just felt so good to cleanse and consolidate. I have been feeling better and more excited about the future and it's just strange.

10 July 2011

Ink born of a freshly brewed thought. Like the coffee I'll have in the morning. What would my high school self say if I told her she'd be drinking red wine alone on a Sunday summer night, reading a book by Stephen King? Me in the present minus my high school self equals what?

I've been having vivid dreams that end right before waking. I'm already different from who I was in Seattle. Now I want…what? I have plans that I fear will fall apart at the slightest touch. My plans have never really been plans. Rather pale, frail-looking excuses for architecture, more like daydreams from the present, attempts at escape from a mundane reality.

16 July 2011

I've been reading *Harry Potter* and lately I have been feeling so jealous of Emma Watson. I wish I could be friends with her or something, because I feel like that would make me feel important somehow, or meaningful, or real. I keep trying to tell myself that she's just a person, it's not like she's better than everyone else. She's just another person. I'm so jealous that she got to be a part of something so beautiful and important. I want to be included. I feel left out and trapped in a place I'm not meant to be.

Lately I've kind of been feeling hopeless and useless, and I can't fully comprehend it. I just want to be a real person and go on adventures and have friends and not feel anxious or have to check in with my parents or worry about money. I am excited for London but terrified of coming back to Boise when it's over. I can't! I will lose what's left of my sanity if I have to come back here.

I don't care about school anymore. I just want to travel and experience things. To be anywhere but here. But I *always* wonder if I'll feel meaningless and unimportant wherever I am. My life is stupid.

Right now I am in Sun Valley with my parents. We are staying in a little townhouse that Dad was able to rent for cheap through his work. Today we rode bikes and hung out. It was beautiful outside. I felt bad for feeling bad, but something's just missing. I'm not where I'm supposed to be.

I've kind of started my period and that may be why I feel weird in a bad way. I feel fat and gross and ugly. Yay, I love being ugly. I am drinking wine and I think it's making it better.

I don't like when my parents are around. I feel like they trap me and that I have to be a certain way when I'm around them and that's not who I really am or want to be. I know they don't mean to do this. It's just how I feel when I'm around them too much. Blah blah blah. What else do I need to say? I feel like there's more but I don't know.

I create daydreams about what London will be like, and about who I'll meet and what we'll do. I think it'll be different from anything I've ever done. Of course it will! I'm so grateful. There will be no expectations, like when I first went to school in Seattle and was expected to play really well and not be able to do my own thing. In London there will be no rules. I'll be able to be a real person and I won't be expected to excel at anything. I think that will make it so much less stressful, and that is hella good.

Oh! I've been thinking about my book again, because I saw that *The Perks of Being a Wallflower* is being made into a movie, and it has been kind of an inspiration for me to write my own book. But guess who is going to be in that movie? EMMA WATSON. GODDD. I am so jealous! She is so cool, and educated, and sophisticated, and talented, and beautiful, and so goddamn lucky. I feel like my life sucks compared to hers. And it does, in reality.

18 July 2011

I rearranged my room again and it looks so spacious! I got rid of more stuff. I don't want anything anymore. I don't want material things, I want to get rid of everything. And it's crazy how much stuff I've already gotten rid of.

Today Mom and I figured out a ton of visa stuff for London, and I also swam at the Y. Kan is coming to visit in about a week! She has a family reunion in Moscow, which is right by Lewiston, so we are going to drive up there and pick her up. I'm so excited!

London London London. Let it be everything I dream of.
Please universe, don't fuck me more than you have already.

24 July 2011

Today I feel stupid. I'm in Lewiston. Mom and I drove up
this morning. Camila and I hung out with Syler and I just felt
disconnected and lame. Like…I am in love with him, but
what are we supposed to talk about when we don't even
really know each other? I just want to make out with him and
touch his body, but it's like I can't do that until we are closer
on a mental and emotional level, and I don't see how that
could ever happen. I can't get close to people unless I spend a
lot of time with them, because I won't trust them *at all* other-
wise. But there's something about Syler. Like, I feel like I
could trust him, it just has to develop?

I guess I just don't understand dating and relationships at all.
Everyone seems to be in a relationship and I just think it's all
so superficial. I don't think a guy will ever understand my
fucked up mind. I also don't understand why any guy would
try. I guess I just think men are kind of useless and I'm frustrated with my desire to be with them and my attraction to
them. They don't understand mental and emotional things. I
have girl friends for that, namely Kan and Zara.

I think I am just confused and frustrated, and probably sexually frustrated, haha. I felt stupid today because I wanted
Syler and I couldn't have him and there was nothing to say
and it was all pointless anyway. I feel like I need a guy in
order to have fun, or at least to be content, and I don't think I
will ever get one because I'm ugly and no guys *ever* like me.
*Ever.** How am I going to never come back to the states if
there's no one to take me away?

120

[*Ana: Guys obviously like you, as you've been with guys before. It's just the guys you idealize and invent in your mind either don't exist or don't know you like them. And probably some of them don't like you back, but that doesn't mean *no* guys like you. –J.]

FUCK MY STUPID, USELESS LIFE. I HATE EVERY-THING, INCLUDING ME.

Is this emotional wreckage?

I don't understand dating. I just do not, and I never will. Unless I can come to terms with my ugly face, stop fearing rejection and embarrassment, and find something goddamn interesting to say. And none of these things will ever happen.

I also don't understand why it is *so uncomfortable* for me to feel stupid, and how easily I start feeling stupid. It makes no sense! I take everything too seriously. I want to leave and never come back. I want to get lost yet feel secure. I want reality, not my mind's twisted perception of it.

You know that feeling you get where you just want to sink into a dark hole, or become so tiny that no one can see you?

I *always* have that feeling.

28 July 2011

Kan visited me in Boise! It felt weird at first but it got way better. We went running at the ski hill close to the city while my parents biked, got drunk with Eli and made ridiculous videos on my laptop, played a shit ton of Wii Mario, and went to the Y. We went downtown and hung out in a coffee shop and talked, and it was so good. I love talking to her, it makes everything okay. We talked about how we felt weird being reunited, and that made it less weird. I took her to the airport yesterday and it was depressing.

29 July 2011

Today sucked because I was bored and wanted to die. I realized that Boise was so much more interesting when Kan was here. Now that she's gone it's awful again.

Blah blah fucking blah.

01 August 2011

Today all I did was see the new *Harry Potter* movie with Mom. I'm also going to go to the Y later. At the end of the movie there was a scene of London, and I just felt so crazy because soon I will be there, and I will touch the buildings with my palms, feel the stone and architecture in person rather than in pictures and my imagination. I got this whoosh of excitement, like things will be okay as soon as I get out of here. There will be importance and meaning, and it will all *matter*.

At night I always create scenes in my head about how London will be, and the people I'll meet, and where I'll go. It makes me nervous and excited. I wish I could keep this feeling for longer than I know it will last. It's so fleeting and I don't think it is supposed to be. That is how I know I'm depressed and anxious. Good feelings, excitement, are always ephemeral. It's weird because I know that when they aren't there I could have them, but I just can't make myself feel that way. It's so fucking weird.

I always think that I would never be able to produce a patronus charm, because when I feel bad I can't conquer it and make myself think about happy or good things. It's like being stuck at the bottom of a well. You can see the light and you know happiness exists, but you just can't get there, especially by yourself.

04 August 2011

I'm in the backyard, it's my favorite weather – completely overcast. Last night Eli came over and we played backgammon, and then watched this show called *Shop Erotic*. It was the funniest thing ever! It's like an infomercial for sex toys. There was this thing called Clone-A-Willy, where you can make a model of anyone's penis! Ha ha ha ha ha what the fuck! Eli thought that was the best thing ever.

I am no longer in the backyard. I am at a coffee shop downtown. I went to this costume store with River, who I haven't seen in a long time, and then sold clothes at a recycled fashion place and made five bucks. I am wearing a long flowery dress.

I talked to Zara on the phone this morning while I was in the backyard – that's why I stopped writing. And I was really anxious about talking on the phone. But I don't think I am anymore.

It's sunnyish now and I want to die. I love the crisp coolness of cloudy, rainy weather. I hope London will be safe. Please let my mind be safe there. I feel like I have things to say but I don't remember what they are. I feel empty.

11 August 2011

I feel kind of anxious right now. Like things aren't right. In a coffee shop, just chillin'. I don't know why I feel weird, like bad things are going to happen. There's a palpability to my emotional contradictions. Vague, abstract, unlearned, real, untruthful, insanity, unfathomable, failure, fuck, fuck it. Too tired to explain what's going on in my life.

Today I was irritable. I went to the dentist and got my crown for my mouth. I have a tooth now, cool.

My period starts next week; I think this is why I am cranky. FML. When this happens I don't feel like doing anything and nothing sounds fun to do. There's no escape from the feelings of futility and boredom and meaninglessness.

I feel satisfied writing in large scrawl. I went to the library downtown today and got two new books. Last night Dad and I watched *Blow*, with Johnny Depp. It was depressing, about drugs and failed relationships and shitty lives. I'm glad I'm not in jail. The movie was long and there was a lot of politics in it, which is often boring to me, so not my favorite movie.

I started transcribing this same diary onto my laptop. Won't it be weird when I finally catch up to myself in the present moment?

I fear commitment. To anything.

15 August 2011

Last night I dreamt about Kurt and Courtney. I played on stage with Kurt and White Lies, and I was playing bass, which I have no idea how to play. Kurt was helping me. He is so beautiful and he has never been mine. Later in the dream I was supposed to take care of Courtney because she was on drugs, but then she turned into this evil uncooperative child. I woke up feeling alone and left out and with a longing to have them be a part of my life, but it'll never happen.

Right now I'm sitting on the front porch in the shade. There's a slight breeze and it's almost cold, or cool. Last night I Skyped Tabby. We have such different lives. She lives, like, an hour away from San Francisco and I am so jealous. I don't think she knows how lucky she is.

Kan told me that today is the first day of preseason practices for soccer, and I am so fucking glad I'm not there and I don't have to do it anymore. I can't express my relief and just plain gratefulness.

I've been pretty bored lately. It's only nice here early in the morning or later when the sun goes down. Everything in between is stiflingly hot and uncomfortable and deserty.

I feel like I'm missing out on so many things in life because I'm antisocial and I live in the middle of nowhere and I'm too anxious about everything. I mean, I'm 20 fucking years old and I've never had sex. But, I also realize that there are millions of people less fortunate than me, and this makes me appreciate what I do have. I'm just never satisfied because I always think about the people that are happier than me, or are doing better things than me.

I always want something better from life, and I don't understand how people settle for things that aren't the best. Like, how can these people be happy when they live in shithole Boise? I don't get it at all. And relationships! How can you have a boyfriend if there are other boys that could be way more awesome?

16 August 2011

Yesterday I hung out with Lisbet. We went to her dad's house because he was having a mini barbecue, and I ate, like, ten of these M&M sugar cookies. I regret doing this. Later we saw *Bridesmaids* and it was so funny!

I dunno how I feel about Lisbet. I kind of get bad vibes from her. I dunno, it's so weird! Because she is into cool things, like good movies that aren't mainstream, and good books and music, but I still get this feeling that she isn't real, or genuine, or that she is judgmental. It's the weirdest thing ever and I don't like it. I feel like I can't talk about real things to her because she'll judge me.

It seems like she has a set right and wrong in her mind and if I do something she considers wrong she'll think I'm stupid, and I don't feel genuine when I'm around her. I kind of don't want to hang out with her anymore. I mean, it wasn't *bad* or *awkward* hanging out with her, it just made me feel anxious and kind of uncomfortable. I feel like there's something about her that isn't right. Maybe it's because I haven't seen her in forever and so it's just strange. Ugh. I don't like this feeling at all.

I want to keep writing forever because it keeps the boredom at bay, but I run out of things to write. Fuck my life. I miss Zara. If she were here we'd be having fun. Or at least hating our lives together. It would be a connection. A real connection between two human minds. That's one of the best things in life. And it's not there when I hang out with Lisbet. I don't know why!

I hate this desert land where everything is far away from everything else. I wish everything was within walking distance of everything else, because it would be so much easier and cheaper to get to places, and I would have more opportunities. More places to go. And I would get more exercise without even trying, because I'd just walk everywhere instead of driving.

Things I want:

A boy to draw me, a messy room, a smaller nose, for Kan to get a new laptop so she can blog to me, to be impulsive, to not be embarrassed to say things I think and feel or to ask for things I want, to be more confident, to not be shy, to be like Courtney Love and tell boys I like them if I do, to not be here, to not be HOT ALL THE TIME IN THE GODDAMN SUN, to find someone that gets it, a boy this time because I have a girl best friend that gets it,

to be the subject of longing, to be the subject of a White Lies song, to be loved by Damon Albarn, to be appreciated by someone of influence, to meet Emma Watson so I can decide for myself if she really is as cool as everyone makes her out to be, to publish this writing right here, for people to see me as genuine, to be the most approachable person ever and for people to know that I'm not judgmental and I want to become friends,

for guys to not only want sex or some shit, for people I don't know to ask me to coffee, for me to not feel threatened by people or to feel that people only want to talk to me because they'll get something out of it, to not feel that people are trying to take advantage of me, to wear awesome fucking outfits, to never come back.

What if the whole world had this connection of understanding? Between every person? A unity. I don't know if that would be a good thing or a bad thing or a weird thing. Hmmm.

Maybe I am judgmental. How can I figure this out?

Things I wish I could do here, but I can't because I live in the suburbs:

ride my bike somewhere cool, walk to a coffee shop, go outside without sweating and wanting to die, people watch, be involved with a guy, go to parties where the people are real, have friends

19 August 2011

Well, yesterday really sucked. I was in the house ALL FUCKING DAY. And bored out of my mind and going insane. But I went to the Y at six with Mom and it was all right. I just hate this place because nothing new ever happens to me and I have nothing new to say. Other than that, I feel like I'm slowly slipping off into a new dimension of insanity.

How do you know things about yourself?

I'm not taking this diary to London. I bought a new one that is very small and has a black leather cover. I love it. I'm thinking about ending my book with this last diary and not including London.*

[*Ana: No, you should definitely include London. –J.]

24 August 2011

Yesterday I texted Syler and told him that I want his body, and he said he didn't want a relationship with me and that he likes me, but things are getting too serious for him. I WAS SO EMBARRASSED!

I've been in Moscow for, like, two days staying with Camila in her apartment. Her university is in Moscow and it's super close to Lewiston. Syler goes to the same university and I slept in his bed *once*. All we did was make out and hump each other. Haha. We hung out and stuff but I didn't act like I wanted to be his girlfriend. I don't even know how to act like

128

that. I just talked to him like I talk to every other human being.

I don't understand why he thought I wanted a relationship when I'm only here for two weeks. I'm going to fucking London! Of course I don't want a relationship! We don't even know each other! I just want his body, and I want to respect him in the way I do everyone else, and I guess he assumed that I wanted something more out of it.

Now that I think about it, we never even talked about anything interesting. Ever. Like, I really do not know who he is at all, or what he believes. I just felt like such an idiot though, because he totally shut me down and I was not expecting that at all. Awkward! I think I'm sexually frustrated because all I want to do is make out with guys.

I think I was excited for Moscow mainly because I knew that Syler would want to make out with me. And he did! He totally initiated the first time we made out. I was reading this magazine on his bed and he sat down next to me and started reading it with me, kind of, and he was really close to my face. He stayed that close to me when we finished reading, so we eventually started kissing.

I seriously have no faith in men and women interacting with each other and being on the same page. Like, I want to hook up with guys, but only if I genuinely like them as people. That doesn't mean that I want them to be the only guy I make out with, and they certainly can kiss other girls. I just want to be genuine and respectful, and I want them to be that way as well.

Do guys only want to fuck and not even talk at all? I want to know what is in their minds, I want to know who they are, and just because I want to know these things doesn't mean I want to be their girlfriend. God, I'm not a fucking object, I'm a person. I don't understand males and I feel stupid.

If we talk again I'm going to explain myself. I'm wondering if he has mental stuff going on. Because he told me he is bipolar, and that's fine. Like, that doesn't bother me at all, but I wonder if that affects his relationships with people to a huge extent. And we do have a relationship, like, as friends, so he shouldn't have used that word, haha. I just don't know what he wants.

Anyway, I've been staying at Camila's apartment in Moscow and it's pretty cool. I brought my own food from home and we also went to the Coop and got food. I've been going to her classes and it's been fun, especially to people watch. So many interesting people, too. I feel like a real person because I don't have to go to soccer practice or anything.

I'm thinking it's good that what happened with Syler happened, because I think I need to experience these things and learn to not feel so stupid so easily. Also, I need to stop fearing rejection, because it wasn't that bad! If I'm not afraid of rejection then I will probably be better at making friends, boy or girl. Okay that is all.

26 August 2011

Lots of things have happened, holy shit. We went to Lewiston the other day and saw Grandma and got Camila's bike and some more of her stuff to bring back to Moscow. We spent the night at Wade's house in Lewiston. Wade is her boyfriend, have I already mentioned him? I slept in his roommate's bed. Josh. He has really long brown hair and I think he is sexy. I peer pressured him into taking shots with me. We were the only ones drinking, it was awesome. We talked all night and he's so fucking cool! And hilarious. And 25. Haha. I think we are going back there tonight and I think everyone is going to drink.

Oh, last night I slept in Bob's bed and we made out. And fooled around. Actually, he just fooled around with me. We didn't have sex though. That is all I'm going to say about that. It was fucked up because he's Camila's ex and apparently I'm not allowed to hook up with him. She is *really* upset with me. I always thought rules like that were dumb. Why would it matter, if they aren't together and she is dating someone else? They haven't been together for more than a year, I think. I don't know, it's weird. Like, he is not even a part of her life anymore. I mean, they are obviously friends but they don't hang out and she has a boyfriend.

But, the whole reason I did that with Bob was because him and Syler are roommates, and Syler and I were hanging out drinking, and I got really drunk and was kind of an asshole to him about the other day when he said he didn't want a relationship. I just called him out on his bullshit and was like, of course I don't want a relationship with you, are you fucking stupid? I called Bob to come get me because he was at a friend's house and in my mind I was like, fuck hanging out with Syler. Bob and I went back to his friend's house, and later when we came back to his and Syler's apartment we hooked up and I slept in his bed. Syler was asleep when we got back so he had no idea.

I think Syler's pissed at me. He has good reason to be. I can't remember exactly what I said to him because I was drunk, but I'm pretty sure I just made him feel really stupid. I don't know. I don't think I care, but I might apologize today through texting. It would be a nice thing to do, I guess.

I feel like such a bad fucking person, though. Camila is so

mad at me, and I feel gross now, too. Fuck my life. The reason I feel bad is because I know that hooking up with Bob really hurt her (well, *now* I know). I would never hurt her on purpose! I know that she is probably telling Wade and his roommates what I did and that I'm an asshole, because I am.

She thinks we had sex even though I told her we just fooled around. She doesn't believe me. I feel like she doesn't understand that the world doesn't obey these unwritten rules about stuff, and that if you fool around with multiple people you aren't evil. I think that creates drama because when people don't obey those rules someone gets pissed. Or hurt, I guess.

I've made out with three different guys this past week (Syler, Josh, Bob) and I don't think that's wrong. My attention is entirely with them when I am with them. I am genuine. I'm not acting like we're dating or something. I want to have a real conversation with them, a legitimate connection. I think that is what a real person would or should do. UGH.

I just feel horrible right now because Camila is so angry with me and I don't know what to do to make it better. I feel like I've overstepped my boundaries since I'm staying with her.

Pain. I'm drunk and it's numbing the pain. I am a bad person. I will never be loved. I am incapable of loving others. I'm too sensitive. How can I tell you everything I feel? How can I be sincere? I have a sick feeling in my stomach. It's a mixture of guilt, shame, regret, and fear. I feel too much of this.

Cutting, pain, skinny, love, music, blood, secrets, fools, mistakes, sensitivity, forgetting, cutting, cutting, regret, alone, silence, wishing you had something you don't, not talking, not being able to trust or confide or talk or love myself, that feeling when you *know* someone thinks you're cool, or beautiful, or inspirational. It's the way they look at you, you can tell. There's a particular feeling, it's real and it exists and I promise I'm not making that shit up I SWEAR.

27 August 2011

Last night we drank and I slept in Josh's bed but we didn't do anything, which is good because I'm totally fucked up. I cried last night because Wade and Camila were fighting about Bob and I felt like it was all my fault. Wade thought that Camila still had feelings for Bob because of how upset she was about me hooking up with him.* Fuck.

[*Ana: Honestly, she's totally overreacting. You're right about the world not following unwritten rules. You shouldn't think you're a bad person for hooking up with him, because how could you have known that she would react this way? If you had known that it would hurt her this badly you wouldn't have done it. –J.]

29 August 2011

a line of sweat, a sliver of shade, watery light, a hard-bound book, broken jewelry, a dying motion, blood all over the walls, uniform structures, indivisible objects, an eternal breath in, imperceptible threads, strings, the vibration of your sound waves, a void never filled, my brain high on abstractions, an infinite cosmos, an unanswerable question, a worthless goal, a self-fulfilling prophecy, a wasted, futile thought, a revolution never formed, your hands clasped, a mind divided, a consciousness warped, a model of the earth, fear of a disease, of no escape, unlimited, open-ended darkness, reason tightened into a fact, a freezing illusion, particles contradicting, violently persuasive concepts, desire as unreliable, consuming sounds, digesting thought, shitting ideas,

Now I desire intoxication but not falsity, truth and genuineness but no commitment, madness and horror but pure sanity, and the mixture of shyness and obnoxiousness.

I feel really misunderstood with Josh. I don't know what his opinion of me is, but I almost think that he doesn't see me as genuine. Sometimes I think he perceives me to be like Camila, and I'm really not like her at all. I am not talkative or social and I don't trust people or open up to them, and I really hate being a part of drama, and I want to escape it when it happens.

The whole Bob situation just made me want to go home. I think I do try to run away from my problems a little bit, and that sucks. I just fucking cannot deal with drama and people that aren't real. I'm not one of those assholes that always creates drama but that always says she hates drama. I really try to not be a part of it and not talk shit about people I like. It's not that hard to not talk shit about your friends!

The other night we went to this girl named Kelsey's house to get drunk. We had gone there once before to drink, and that first time we were there I ate a cookie I found in the kitchen and used some nail polish I found in the bathroom. When we went there again Camila told me that Kelsey was pissed about me doing that stuff, and hated me because of it. Camila was really mean about it, like, she just kept saying that I shouldn't touch other people's shit, and making it sound like I was a horrible person that kept ruining her relationships with people, and that I really fucked up.

It hurt so badly. I cried on the back steps by myself. But, Kelsey hates Camila anyway because Camila is dating Wade and Kelsey likes Wade apparently. I dunno, it just fucking sucked and was dramatic and irrational and I hated it. Camila was so mean about it! We made up because she realized I didn't even do anything wrong, because who gives a shit if I used someone's nail polish? That's the fucking dumbest thing I've ever heard. And really immature. So Kelsey can suck my huge fat cock.

It was just a mind fuck because Camila doesn't even like Kelsey but she was still being rude to me and saying I shouldn't touch Kelsey's stuff. Wade came out back and consoled me, and Camila and I made up and it all ended up being okay. But, what the fuck? Just more drama that made me want to go home. I feel like I don't have the energy to respond to this kind of behavior; it's pointless.

It was better when we went back to Wade's house because Josh and I took more shots and acted ridiculous and it was fun. Wade and Camila went to bed and I slept in Josh's bed and we kissed. I like it because we don't really make out; it's basically me just kissing him on the lips multiple times. It's an expression of shy affection and I like how that makes me feel.

We watched a documentary about The Doors, which is a band I want to get into. I just think Josh is so fucking cool, and I want him to think of me as a real person, but I'm not sure if he does. If I lived here I would want him to be my boyfriend. Because he talks! Like, he asks me questions about myself and he tells me about his life and his childhood and I think that is so interesting. Other people aren't like that!

I haven't talked to Syler or Bob since the night Bob and I hooked up.

I think I figured out Camila, and why she is mean to me sometimes. I'm pretty sure it's jealousy. Because I'm good at sports and (apparently) I have a nice body, and other stuff that she might be jealous of, I don't know. But I think that she feels threatened by me coming here because she doesn't want her friends to like me more than her, which they probably don't anyway! Because that's the one thing she really has going for her – social stuff, relationships, likability, FRIENDS. That stuff is definitely not my forte. But if I do better than her in that area, or if her friends express that they like me or think I'm cool or attractive, she feels taken advantage of or used or threatened, because that is her territory.

And I love her, and I know she loves me, but I don't think I can trust her as much as I'd like anymore, just because I know she talks to a ton of people and she would probably tell Wade all of my secrets…maybe not, I dunno. I'm starting to realize that she really doesn't understand my mind on a fundamental level. I don't think she will ever be able to, just because of differing personality characteristics, different brain chemistry. It's weird and it makes me uneasy because we grew up together, kind of, and I have always imagined her as being one of the people closest to me.

I've been anxious because I keep expecting Camila to get pissed at me for doing something disrespectful that I didn't know was disrespectful, or crossing some line I didn't know I shouldn't have crossed, or didn't know was even there. You can tell that she has issues with personal space. I can see how she would think that I'm taking advantage of her if I do some small thing. Like make out with one of her friends, or use one of her roommate's things.

It reminds me of soccer in Seattle. I became immobile and anxious because I couldn't figure out what to do that would make Chadwick the least angry. And it's like everything I do is wrong and makes someone angry. It's such a strange situation and it's not fun to be in. What you think is okay to do may not be okay with someone else, and it creates this horrible uncertainty that stops all desire to move.

30 August 2011

This is the diary of Ana.

All I want is a tall, super thin notebook with no spirals, so that I can share a consciousness bloated with poetry and strung out on vowels. I want you to see it, I want you to know.

I love the "On Melancholy Hill" lyrics by Gorillaz. I'm so in love with that song.

Today wasn't too productive. I read some, ate a shit ton and I am unhappy about it, and also went shopping for a notebook, which I didn't find. I am currently writing in one of Camila's notebooks that she didn't want.

I feel like throwing up. I haven't worked out in forever and it makes me want to sleep and/or die.

When I get bored I want to form new sentences, or get fucking wasted and like myself.

This may be real life, is this what I expected?

I will never be happy wherever I am; I will always want to be somewhere else. My knee hurts and I'm bored.

31 August 2011

Yesterday I ate a ton of shit. I think it was because I was anxious and bored, and I'm really mad at myself for doing that. It was panic, maybe.

We came back to Lewiston from Camila's apartment in

Moscow and stayed at Wade's apartment again. I slept in Josh's bed, as usual. This time I was super anxious and I never talked first. He is so fucking good at saying the right thing, and starting conversations, and asking questions. So it ended up being okay. But I still think he is misunderstanding my mind and my intentions, and that makes me feel weird and want to explain myself, but it's really hard.

I told him that I have an avoidant personality and that's probably why I only have three friends. Which was an exaggeration, obviously. Although I do consider my friend list as quite low. I think he misunderstood my definition of friend. He was giving me a hard time for not considering him to be my friend, which I don't. KIND OF. I just can't figure out what a friend is, because I feel like it's someone that I would hang out with a lot and that understands my mind (at least a little bit), which would make my friend list as follows: Eli, Camila, Kan, Zara.

I feel like if I don't know someone really well and haven't spent a bunch of time with them, and have not gotten to the point where I don't feel awkward *at all*, then they aren't really my friend. They're just an acquaintance. A friend would be someone I would consider texting or calling, which I don't usually do. There is a short list of people that I would contact first, and those people are my friends. All others are acquaintances or potential friends.

It just takes a lot of time, because I don't trust people or open up to people very quickly. I opened up to Josh and I don't know why. I think I can tell right away who potential friends are, and it's just easier for me to open up to them. That's how a friendship occurs or grows into something that I would consider to be meaningful or important. Does anyone else feel this way? Jesus.

I don't understand what the point of hanging out with someone is if you aren't going to create a connection in your mind, if you aren't going to figure out yourself in relation to them, or become closer to them. I would never ask certain people on my college soccer team to hang out, or Calvin, or most of the guys on the soccer team, or Camila's roommates, or fucking Davis! I know already that they don't get it, that they don't understand how my mind works or the concepts that fuel my desires, and because of this I have no desire to hang out with them. Sure, they are "friends," like, I've hung out with them and we are on good terms, but I wouldn't care if I never saw them again, and I wouldn't contact them.

I think I am completely crazy.

I also feel stupid, kind of, when around Josh, because I feel like he thinks I'm mentally fucked and unstable, which I kind of am, but I don't want him to know that right away, you know? I wonder if I told him too much, too soon. I don't know why I am even thinking about this because I am leaving Moscow and Lewiston in a week and I'll probably only see him one more time before then. And then never again. Whatever.

01 September 2011

I worked out today for the first time since I've been here, and I felt SO good afterwards, unbelievable. Now we're drinking before the tailgate because there is a football game today. Camila only tailgates, she doesn't go to the games.

I took a shit because of the alcohol, and I feel good about myself. It's weird how that works out. Just a small shift in brain chemicals and I feel okay. Weird. I've never drank alcohol in the daytime before, so it's a new experience, and I love new experiences. Why don't I always feel this good? I'll never know.

You know what? This is how weird I am. I am in Camila's room writing this journal entry while drunkish and everyone else is in the living room talking and drinking and being normal people. I felt the urge for pencil and paper and documentation. Why don't others feel this urge?

This pencil glides gracefully between atomic blue fences.

02 September 2011

Yesterday I went to bed at, like, 8:45 p.m., haha. We drank for most of the day and never ended up going to the tailgate, which didn't bother me. I just love being drunk, it's a beautiful adventure. When I go home I know I'll be wondering what Camila is up to, and I am glad that I know now. I don't think her life is as exciting as I always picture it to be, which is cool. For me. Ha. I just like knowing that I'm not really missing out on anything, at least anything that I'd be dying to do. Camila has always had this vibe of "being where it's at," in my mind.

London, London, London. Today was a day of survival, of running, of books and clothes and hunger, of baggy shirts and braided hair, of money and plans and thoughts of home and the future, of movies and studies and writing. All of these things I love. I love all the feelings they entail and all the vibes swirling around these objects and ideas.

I want to go on runs in London and see everything, and take a new route every day. I want a boyfriend from London who can take me everywhere, show me the fuckin' ropes or whatever. Because I want to see everything, I want to know everything there is to know. I need a tour guide.

Today we didn't do anything, it was lame. Right now Camila is drinking at some frat. I didn't feel like it. I felt like being alone and writing, and I'm glad I didn't go. I'm watching the same documentary about The Doors that Josh and I watched in his bed while drunk. I think Jim Morrison is sexy because he was so fucking intelligent and thought about revolutionary concepts and ended up killing himself. I think he killed himself?

Anyway, we didn't go back to Lewiston today like we had initially planned because we don't have a car anymore, so Wade would have to come get us. But he wouldn't come get us, and the reason why is because apparently Josh wanted to fuck some other girl and they didn't want me to feel bad or something. Oh, my god. I don't care if he fucks some other girl, it's not like we're dating! We didn't even have sex!

They are so goddamn dramatic it annoys the shit out of me!! I guess it might have felt awkward because there'd be nowhere for me to sleep. I could have slept with Wade and Camila, though. Or on the couch, or on the ground. I don't know, whatever. WHO CARES!? Why do they think I have rights to Josh or something? He can do whatever the fuck he wants. Jesus. I am not one of them, I don't think the way they think.

There will be no truth, loyalty, honesty, purity. Only drama, deceit, lies, jealousy. Men and women cannot mingle without pain.

I can't stop eating because I am so bored. It's just Camila and I in her apartment and there is nothing to do and I'm going crazy. Wade may or may not come get us. I just want to die. I'm in one of those moods where nothing in the whole world sounds like fun. Eating is the only thing that is slightly pleasurable. Maybe I'll cut myself, that's always interesting. Camila is on the phone with Wade. We have no more fake sugar for coffee. I think I'll read my book, which has actually started to bore me.

Things I want:

To be legitimately hungry, to have an infinite array of activities to do, to wear many different outfits, to have an apartment alone, to have a closet of only my favorite things, for it to be slightly cold so I can wear layers and dark lipstick and appear sultry and mysterious, to never have cravings, to smoke off the balcony, to never be bored, to have friends in London, to be special and important, to read poetry and smoke cigarettes in outdoor cafes, to be sincere.

I know I look cool and people want to know who I am. I need to use this to my advantage, I need to take control. I need to bring my fisheye camera everywhere, I need them to look at me, I need their attention. I need power and beauty and blood and black nail polish and caressing the words on the pages of the novels I inhabit.

Poetry, heat, silky fabrics, travel and luggage and beauty products, pencil lead, paper, paperback books you can bend to your will, sea horses on skinny arms, déjà vu, movies, braids, watercolors,

06 September 2011

I'm *finally* back home, it is amazing. I feel like I stayed in Moscow for too long, because this past weekend when I was there we didn't do anything. I ate too much and wanted to die of boredom. It's funny because one of the reasons I was so excited to go to Moscow initially was Syler. I totally thought we were going to have this awesome two-week fling, and I kind of wanted to lose my virginity. Isn't it weird how reality never coincides with your desires?

Instead he decided that things were getting too "serious" so I hooked up with his roommate instead! Isn't that bad? Especially because it was fucking *Bob*, Camila's ex. Whoops. I didn't touch his dick, and we didn't have sex, but he did touch me. A lot. Fuck. It was a bad decision but I'm glad it happened because I learned a lot from it, like what not to do…

Bob told me that I am "ripped," and that made me feel so fucking good about myself, you don't even know. It was in reference to my stomach and I HATE my stomach!! Then a couple days later Josh said something along those lines, I think while we were drunk. He asked if I had to do a ton of sit-ups. Which I do. But I seriously was so happy I can't explain. I think guys don't notice your imperfections, they just see a general idea when they look at your body. Because I honestly don't think I have a great stomach; I've hated it for years.

And I do not think my face is pretty at all, but I'm starting to have a sneaking suspicion that guys might. Because at the Saturday market in Moscow this guy started a conversation with me about my fisheye camera, and then when I left he was totally staring at me. I had my sunglasses on so he didn't know I could see him.

I love when people watch me. It's the greatest thing ever. I think that because I am insecure about my body and face, I like to see people admire it from afar or when I am wearing something cool. But I won't ever let anyone see me when I get out of the shower. Because my hair is all slicked back and I look horrible. Or when I really need to wash my face, like after I wake up and am greasy. I hate those moments. I dunno, I think I just like attention because it makes me feel important and influential.

08 September 2011

Today I had an orthodontist appointment and they put a permanent retainer on my bottom teeth. Thank god! Now I don't have to wear my bottom retainer.

After that I went to the mall to look for running shoes to take to London. I want some that could be fashionable as well, so that I could wear them while exploring or just in my daily life. Because one of my biggest pet peeves is when people wear ugly running shoes with their outfit, like, with jeans. Why does anyone think that's okay? Running shoes are fugly, and I am going to find good looking ones if it's the last thing I do.

When I was at the mall I went into a shoe store, and the guy there started a conversation with me. I told him my life story. Well, just where I went to school and that I'm going to London. He was gross though, haha. I felt like I had to stay there and talk to him even when I didn't find any shoes that I wanted. And then I said, "Okay, see you later…" but he kept talking. And then he awkwardly walked away without saying bye. I feel like lately I have been making guys feel awkward and I love it, because it makes me feel powerful. Like, I think I made the guy at Saturday market feel awkward, and I was like, "Yeah, bitch, I did that." Ha.

I like my hair today because I braided it last night and slept in it, so today it's curly and messy. Like bedhead hair. I love that. I love that on guys. Boys with long hair, where are you?

I have started being annoyed with myself when journaling because I feel like I'm writing for other people instead of myself, since I want to get this published for other people to read. Like, I feel like I start phrasing things differently or something. I don't know. I'll be glad when I go to London and end the part of my diaries that will be included in my book, because they'll be mine again, and secret.

If I ever do get this published and you are reading this right now, I would like to say hello. It's like when people write letters to their future children. Which I personally think is creepy. Fuck you, that's what I say to my future children. Good thing I'm not having any.

I'm drinking coffee on the front porch. Yesterday I rearranged my whole room, it looks hella tite. I feel like a real person. I love seeing other people's rooms because it's such an insight into who they really are. And it makes them so real. I think I feel real when I like my room, because it makes me feel towards myself the way I feel towards other people when I see their rooms. Like Weston. And Mila's room at the Brick. And Kan's dorm freshman year. And Sawyer's room in college when we went to his graduation. All real.

09 September 2011
Good things now:

My life is plump and ripe with opportunity. I like my bedhead hair and my outfits and the boiling water tap in the kitchen and Reese's Puffs cereal and watching movies and having my mattress on the floor and late nights looking at London maps and trying to figure out where everything is.

Documents and instructions and imagining what it will be like and websites and pictures and creating scenarios in my head that I'd die for because I want them so much.

Tomorrow we are driving a few hours to Idaho Falls to bury Grandpa's ashes. It's just a small family thing. I am excited to get up early and drink coffee and listen to music in the car.

I leave for London in 16 days, I think.

10 September 2011

This morning we woke super early and drove to Idaho Falls. I slept most of the way so it wasn't bad. Today was kind of boring but it was all right. It was basically just hanging out with Dad's side of the family and friends of my grandparents. I felt kind of awkward but not really. I just feel awkward at the goodbye stage because you have to hug everyone but you don't really know them, so I just feel weird. Because I'm not close to Dad's side of the family like I am with Mom's.

We ate dinner at some people's house that were friends with my grandparents. It was totally fine. I ate probably too many cupcakes, but it's okay because I worked out when we got back to our hotel and I did a billion sit ups. Tomorrow we are getting up hella early again and driving home.

Grandma (Mom's side) is coming for a couple days and she'll be at our house by around noon tomorrow, I think.

12 September 2011

Today I got up at seven to say goodbye to Grandma and my aunt. They only stayed for one day. I wish they could have stayed for longer.

I'm scared I'm one of those people that won't work hard in order to accomplish a goal. I'm afraid I'll never publish my book because I'll just give up when it gets difficult. This makes me feel so fucking uneasy. About myself, about life. I start feeling this way and then I freeze up and I don't feel like doing anything and I can't remember all the quotes I write down that make me feel better, or the people or the music or the feelings that are good and that push me along. It's so weird.

I feel hopeless but I know it'll pass soon. I just feel like it's going to be so hard to get published, and be a fucking annoyingly long process, and that just makes me want to give up, but I know I can't.

Just feeling that desire scares the shit out of me because I don't want to be the kind of person that gives up when things get difficult. That's why quitting soccer had such a huge impact on me and made me really confused about and hate myself. Because soccer was my whole life. I don't even remember starting to play soccer, that's how young I was when I started.

I guess I don't really know what kind of person I am. I mean, I do, I just am unsure a lot and change my mind a lot.

13 September 2011

I need to calm the fuck down I need to slow down. I need to eat slower. I need to stop thinking of all the shit I have to do because it overwhelms me. I need to stop trying to get the best deal, or the best option, because it's exhausting. Try to get a good deal, but don't freak out about it because it's not worth freaking out about! Balance. Last night I was really worried and I think these things contributed to that.

Jenna is going to be here this weekend because her sister is getting married, so hopefully I'll get to see her before I disappear forever. God, it's so weird. She was my best friend growing up and I rarely see her anymore. It's just so fucking crazy that we aren't the neighborhood kids anymore. I always see kids playing in our neighborhood and I think about how that used to be my best friend and I and other random friends.

It's time. I think about how kids are going to my high school right now, and I never have to do that again. Like, right now, this very fucking moment, there are teenagers slaving away in that awful jail, and I am not one of them. Do you feel the beauty in that? Do you understand how happy that makes me? Not that they are suffering, but that I don't have to anymore. It just blows my mind. Growing up is strange as fuck.

15 September 2011

Today is cool and overcast and there's a soft breeze. It makes me think about change and the future, and I get excited to do new things and go to new places. I also am nervous because I'll be living on my own and I'll have to buy my own food and support myself. Which will be fine, it's just weird because I've never had to buy my own food. I think I'll be a real person.

You know, London is the largest city in Europe and has a population of 7.56 million. HOLY FUCK. That is so many people! I think I like that but I am not sure. I do.

I was weighing my suitcase yesterday and it was so fucking heavy so I have to bring a second one so I don't get overweight baggage fees. I feel like I'm bringing too much, but a lot of it I will be using up and throwing away when I'm done with it, like toiletries. I dunno. I don't want to be that one person that packs way too fucking much and looks ridiculous and doesn't use all the stuff they bring. But it's for, like, nine months! Anyway, it will be an adventure and a trip of discovery.

I am reading a book called *Futureproof* by N. Frank Daniels, and I really like it. It kind of makes me anxious because the kids in it do *so many* drugs. I feel anxious about drugs because they make me think about insanity and I'm terrified of insanity. I feel bad for those kids because they are poor and their lives are shitty. I feel guilty for having good relationships with my family and still being depressed and anxious and confused and hating myself. I don't really have a reason to feel that way, and those kids do, in my mind.

I think so many stories are written for the kids who are poor and have shitty family situations, so I want my book to be for the kids who should be fine, but aren't. The kids who are too afraid to do drugs because of insanity and getting too into their own minds, who are confused and without purpose and want to hit bottom but are too afraid to do that, too, because it means losing everything. Maybe they are too attached to things, which makes them uncomfortable as well.

I just don't feel safe around drugs because you aren't you when you take them, and all I want is truth and genuine people. If I do drugs I become way more confused and introspective than normal, and that gets bad. I dunno. Let's not talk about it anymore.

20 September 2011

Haven't written for a while. I caught up to myself transcribing this onto my laptop and it made me weird so I stopped writing. Yesterday was Mom's birthday, so she took work off and we ran a shit ton of errands, which is what we always do together.

Last night I put, like, 80 fake tats on. Okay, I put on nine. There is a special place in my heart for fake tattoos. How could one not love them?

I finished my book and I started another called *Bad Marie*. It's okay. Somehow it feels cliché, and I get the same vibe I got from my writing professor who was annoying to me. Like weird hipster wannabe starving artist writer. A poser. Ha! A poser! Omg I haven't heard that word in so long! That was, like, seventh grade, haha.

Sawyer is supposed to come home this week! Him and Lacy got back to Seattle yesterday, which is where Lacy's family lives. They said they saw a fat, Asian version of me in the airport. My clone, except Asian and overweight. Wtf? Sawyer is coming back here while Lacy tries to get a job in Seattle.

I leave for London in seven days. On Sunday morning, early. I am nervous about meeting people. I hope my roommate is nice. I hope it all works out.

Last night I dreamt that ants were getting in my toothbrush. In the electric toothbrush head. I also had another anxiety dream about Chadwick and soccer, which is what I've been having nightmares about lately. Post traumatic stress disorder? Kan's going to quit soccer after school starts, I dunno if I've already mentioned that. But she wants to leave school after first quarter and come to London with me and never come back. We are Kana, we are invincible. We are forever.

I'm sitting on the porch drinking coffee. It's getting progressively cooler here. It's actually chilly when you first step outside into the shade. I have a sweater and a hot drink, so it's okay.

There's so much history all around us. We are only pieces in a game of time, to be manipulated and burnt out in any possible moment. But, London! London has so much history and I want to know it all. Like fucking Shakespeare's Globe. I can't even comprehend. It just blows my mind. How am I supposed to feel?

I think that my time here has been way more enjoyable knowing that I'm leaving, and being busy getting my shit together in order to leave. It's weird. I just feel like these past couple weeks haven't been shittily boring. I am excited to get rid of this diary. I mean, store it away and start fresh, because it feels cleansing. I get to start a new life and forget the shit that came before, and I think that will be nice.

23 September 2011

London is the day after tomorrow. I am so nervous. I dyed my hair blue, purple, pink, and a little bit of black the other day. It looks hella good. Nothing else. I feel weird knowing that I'm leaving and not knowing what to expect. I won't know anyone. It's just strange knowing you are going to have to adapt soon, but not knowing how, or what exactly will happen. It's exciting but scary. Intriguing.

I am going to bed now, I guess, if I can calm down. Goodnight.

author's note

27 August 2020

You are the vast, infinite darkness I fear and long for. Fuck me up, baby, show me your face. Show me your three-dimensional manifestations. Scare me, then I will know you are truly here.

I want to feel like I'm hallucinating and have it be real. I want to feel true awe, my heart beating faster, thumping my ribcage. You can taste my fear but it's only painful desire for things I'll never have.

I'm your slave, I make you offerings at midnight. I'll wait for you during your hour, face turned toward the heavens, expectant, willing, waiting.

I'll wait for you forever because you are the only one. Only you can make me happy because you are immortal, Timeless, ancient wisdom hidden just out of reach, synchronicities involving death, a magician's fantasies of controlling powerful, pulsing energy, a heavy gravitational force pulling me towards you, tightening my coils, three crows staring me in the eyes and chanting to me, strange friendships with insects, sprouting mushrooms covered in black slime, Quality, an eery obsession with Self, love and hatred in the same moment, scrambling spider feet, a desperation for control that must be unlearned, experience, a tightened anxiety grip, sun-bleached bones, the Devil card reversed, a carefully managed marijuana addiction,

an uncomfortable limbo that is my life, the edge of everything, the exception to every rule, the boundary between what I hate and what I want, easy communication with felines, never belonging, always on the outside looking in — even when I'm really on the inside, peering around corners, being misunderstood by those who will never understand, the art of planting secrets that go unnoticed, shadowy solitude, desiring invisibility,

me dressed in black, lighting candles, reading aloud from the Picatrix.

Forever yours,
J. Guzmán

if you enjoyed this book

If you enjoyed this book I would love your feedback in the form of a short review. **Your comments are valuable and extremely appreciated, and will help me out on my indie author career path!!**

Follow me on Instagram @jguzmanwriter or visit my website jguzman.space. There you can sign up for my mailing list under the Contact tab.

Made in the USA
Monee, IL
01 February 2022